RAMON, MARIA AND THEIR NEIGHBORS

STORIES FROM RURAL VENEZUELA IN THE 1950s

JOHN HENDERSON SINCLAIR

Manufactured in the United States of America

10 9 8 7 6 5 4 3 2 1

The paper used in this publication meets the minimum requirements of the American National Standard for Information Services – Permanence for Printed Library Materials, ANSI Z.39.48 – 1984

The author has received permission from Antonio Rivero and Richard L.Turner, Jr. for the printing of their paintings and photographs in this book.

International Standard Book Number
ISBN 978-0-692-01811-8
Library of Congress Control Number : 2012941017

PREFACE

As I write in the second decade of the 21st century, I recall the world of the 1950s, now six decades ago, when I was still in my twenties!

I have tried to weave together my memories of the people I came to know and love in rural Venezuela years ago. Our family was privileged to share in the lives of wonderful people there. Their lives impacted and enriched our lives in our young adult years. All this transpired at the beginning to the nuclear age and before humans had invaded outer and cyberspace. It was the epoch of East-West confrontation which seemed to challenge the so-called "free world".

Still the people with whom our lot was cast for a short time in our lives were the same people as today – some loveable and others more difficult to love. Some neighbors were more open to new ideas than others who perceived new ideas a threatening. Yet all of us are children of God and loved equally by Our Creator.

I write from the perspective of an American missionary whose intention was to become a friend to the friendless and a pastor to those who had no shepherd. I wanted to be a purveyor of hope in their lives and society. Our efforts may well have been tangential to what transpired in their lives and nation, but for me, my wife and sons, the journey through Latin lands was life transforming.

In writing this book, I have been resourced by missionary and national church colleagues with whom we served in rural Venezuela: the Reverend Robert E. Seel, the Reverends Carlos and Deborah Clugy-Soto, the Reverend Eugene W. Lee and his wife, Jeanne Marie.

I am in debt to those Venezuelan friends and colleagues who received and trusted us as friends. We were blessed by their friendship and companionship. This book is a small down payment on that debt.

Above all I am indebted to my beloved wife and co-workers in mission, Maxine Banta Sinclair, and our sons, David, Paul and John Mark for their unending love and support in my missionary calling.

John H. Sinclair, September, 2012

FOREWARD

I remember the author, John H. Sinclair, from when I was a teenager. My father and other people in the church in Caracas told me that he was a missionary to the "campesino" communities of the Tuy Valley in the State of Miranda. The image I first formed of him was of "a North American farmer pastor" riding a mule with a group of peasants in the impoverished rural areas.

Years later during my theological studies at Princeton Theological Seminary, my wife Donna and I visited him in his office in the Presbyterian mission board in New York City. He was then the Regional Secretary for Latin America and the Caribbean. I wondered how this refined executive could be the same man who rode a mule with "campesinos" in the Tuy Valley! About that same time we met his mother, a delightful lady from Scotland who lived in the same community as Donna's mother in East Stroudsburg, Pennsylvania. We learned from her that her son had not grown up in a rural area, but in a small town in Kansas.

Upon our return to Venezuela, we came to know the congregations in Santa Barbara and Ocumare. We met the Lara and Esinpoza families and knew Ramon and Maria. I realized that Pastor Sinclair had to learn a lot about rural life to be able to identify with them and their lives. He and his wife, Maxine, became a beloved pastor and friend to these country folk. They embraced their missionary calling with great love. The Gospel was preached by word and deed in the concrete situations which those impoverished people faced. Hope was brought to people who had little hope. Salvation was announced in the midst of darkness.

Venezuela today is a very different country from the one the Sinclairs found in 1950. A revolutionary process is under way. Social, economic and cultural transformations are taking place at a tremendous speed. In this excellent book, "RAMON, MARIA AND THEIR NEIGHBORS: Stories from rural Venezuela in the 1950s", the author poses key questions for the Christian churches in Venezuela in the present moment: Are we to support the Bolivarian revolution? Can we embrace the 21st century Socialism which Hugo Chavez is promoting? What is the specific mission of the church today in our nation? How can we present a prophetic witness in the midst of the present situation?

The example of this missionary couple, those who preceded them and those who followed them, can serve as a guide for us today. We are called to embrace the Gospel with great love and to become one with the people in their search for freedom and justice. We are called upon to proclaim the Gospel with a prophetic voice in the daily situations which our congregations face in our society. Our actions must show that Christ continues to be our hope and our salvation.

The Rev, Dr. Edgar Moros Ruano is an ordained minister of the Iglesia Evangelica Presbiteriana de Venezuela and pastor of the congregation "La Resurrecion" in Merida. He is a graduate of Maryville College, Princeton Theological Seminary and holds a doctor of philosophy from Vanderbilt University. He and his wife, Donna, have also served in theological education in Spain, Colombia and Venezuela under the Presbyterian Church, USA mission board. In addition to his pastoral duties, he teaches philosophy at the Universidad de Los Andres and has been involved in research projects related to the Protestant churches in Venezuela.

DEDICATORY

To my beloved wife, Maxine, and our three sons, David, Paul and John Mark (*)

(*) This photo was taken in 1954. Our youngest son, John Mark, was born in Chile in 1957.

PROLOGUE

In the beginning of the 21st century, Venezuela, a land barely known except for its oil reserves appeared on the stage of democracy. The voice of the poor masses of Venezuela was finally heard. This new cry for political , social, and economic justice from a people so long disempowered brought new hope to their world, in much the same way as the Cuban revolution became a beacon of hope for the masses in Latin America during the later years of the 21st century.

But what is the story behind the story of the Venezuela project in 2012? Unlike most countries in the region, for the last 50 years, Venezuela had lived through an uninterrupted "democratic period" of rule by two political parties. Similar to the political system of the USA, both parties have generally served the interests of the economic elites which showed only marginal concern for the masses who lived in dire poverty.

What could the impoverished masses learn from the Old Testament story of their exodus from the Egypt of oppression and their journey to "the promised land" ? Was their dream of freedom only an illusion?

This is a story about a spiritual renewal through religious faith and the relation of that faith to the development of authentic democracy. The backlands of the State of Miranda had long been a private fiefdom of the privileged economic elites of Caracas when the Gospel arrived there in the 1920s. Did anything really change?

Religion has always been an essential component in the character of society. The freedom to propagate one's religious belief is a prerequisite to authentic democracy. In large measure, Venezuela has enjoyed much religious freedom for all its citizens. There was fertile soil in the Upper Tuy Valley for radical change,even in the 1950s.

Fast forward to 2012

A new model of democracy and self-determinism of Hugo Chavez

Frias is bringing about profound changes today in Venezuelan society However, these stories set in the 1950s, was a different chapter in the struggle of the people of Venezuela for a better life for themselves and their children.

Hugo Chavez Frias, a self-identified indigenous Venezuelan, has remained popular among the people and at the same time is garnering increased attention by the international community. Only time will tell if his regime will succeed or if it will become another populist government in the political history of Latin America.

What are the new factors present today which were not present in the 1950s?

1. The significant population growth of the 1960s through 2011 and the rapid urbanization of Venezuela.

2. Several political movements in Latin America in recent years have succeeded in building more stable democracies.

3. There is a development in many churches of a more progressive social agenda. This is especially true of the Roman Catholic Church which has moved away slowly from captivity by the oligarchy, the military and the landed gentry.

4. The economy of Latin America in the world economy is more significant. For example, the economy of Brazil has now replaced France as the fifth largest economy. The region is no longer seen only as a source of cheap, raw materials for the developed world but it has emerged as one of the leading economies the world.

5. The Protestant community in Latin America is showing more maturity in understanding the relation between faith and freedom.

TABLE OF CONTENTS

PART ONE

VENEZUELA - "The Little Venice"

Place, people and culture

VENEZUELA – "Little Venice"

The northern coast of the South American continent was inhabited by indigenous people as early as the second millennium B.C. It was not until Christopher Columbus arrived in 1492 that the history of Latin America began to be recorded.

One of the most picturesque villages at the edge of the modern city of Maracaibo (population 1, 250,000) is Santa Rosa de Agua. Today there is little to show of the original village which was visited by the navigators Alonso de Ojeda, Amerigo Vespucci and Juan de la Cosa when they traced the coastline in 1498 of the region known today as Venezuela.

In the feverish minds of the early explorers, the comparison of the likeness of this village to the noble city of Venice, is understandable. From this lyrical comparison, human in expression and universal in history, came the name of the nation - Venezuela or "Little Venice". In practical terms, the ancient village was born out of necessity to defend the inhabitants from the animals and insects! Such were the humble beginnings of Venezuela.

Venezuela suffering initially because of its geographic location. The rich and populous part of the land was a narrow strip along the sea. There the peaks and valleys make for a pleasant climate, but access to the ocean was only possible through the mountain passes. However the greater barrier to growth was the lack of immigration and the new ideas these immigrants brought from the outside world.

Today a powerful nations with the capital city of Caracas, with a population of over 3,089,000 (2010) in the metropolitan area, plays a leading role in Latin America with its industry, commerce, education and culture. Today the *mestizos* are the majority of the population, with perhaps ten percent white, ten percent negroid and less than five percent indigenous.

Mountains and plains dominate the geography of Venezuela. The Orinoco River system covers practically the entire country and includes an extended and thickly wooded area. The *llanos* (plains) occupy one-third of the country's central region.

Venezuela has been described as having four parts: The northwest is a prolongation of the Andes Mountains where the large cities of Caracas, Valencia and Merida are situated; to the west of Caracas is the Maracaibo basin with the vast reserves of oil. 90% of the population resides in these two areas; the third area is the plains or "los llanos", known also as the Orinoco Basin ; and the fourth area is the Guyana Highlands on the far east.

The principal mineral resources of the nation include iron, gold, bauxite and diamonds. The resources of petroleum and natural gas are among the most abundant of any nation. Agricultural products are sugar, coffee, cacao, corn and bananas.

A culture of authoritarian leadership

It has been said that in the early years of the Province of Gran Colombia (Ecuador, Colombia and Venezuela) that Ecuador was a convent, Colombia was a university and Venezuela was a military garrison! Certainly Venezuela has had it share of military dictators. The nation has survived over fifty military revolts and written twenty constitutions.

Military strong men ruled the country from 1830 . There were four dominant personalities between 1830 and 1935: Jose Antonio Paez (1830 – 1887); Antonio Guzman Blanco (1870 – 1888); Cipriano Castro (1899 – 1908); and Juan Vicente Gomez (1908 – 1935). The military dictators were finally overthrown when General Marcos Perez Jimenez was ousted in 1958. There was only a brief period of democracy between 1935 and 1959). A new constitution was adopted in 1961 which marked the beginning of authentic democracy. Venezuela has experienced great economic prosperity because of its natural resources for decades until it began to experience an economic decline in the 1990s.

The overthrow of General Gomez

A cadre of new leaders emerged known as "The Class of 1929", a title given to a group of university graduates who were determined to make the dream of an independent, democratic nation become a reality.. Among those visionary young leaders were Romulo Betancourt and Romulo Gallegos. One leader was the reformed- minded General Lopez Contreras, the military leader who sided with these youthful reformers.. He formed a government in 1936 which implemented many reforms, one being land redistribution..

The State of Miranda

The Federal District is surrounded on three sides by the large rural State of Miranda. Before 1936 most of the land was owned by the military and business elites of Caracas. These families spent their weekends in their country homes, returning with grain, fruit and vegetables which the *campesinos* had produced on their land. The peasants could keep a portion of the crops as "payment" for their labor. Other employees were known as *medianeros* who agreed to turn over to the owners a specific percentage of their crops.

There were eleven villages in the state: Ocumare, Guarenas, Guatire, Higerote, Rio Chico, Cua, Charallave, Paracotos, Yare, Santa Teresa, Santa Lucia and the capital, Los Teques with a population of about ten thousand.

The Mendoza Rural Development Project

A vast extension of fertile farm land in the Upper Tuy Valley which had been the feudal estates of the military elites of General Gomez was expropriated. The are was about one hundred square miles along both banks of the Tuy River between Cua and Ocumare. – villages at either end of the valley. Between these two towns were scattered a dozen of more *poblaciones* or neighborhoods. One was the Santa Barbara "colony" with fifty or more huts, two *bodegas* (small stores) and two *hacienda* houses.

The majority of the inhabitants in the southern half of the State of Miranda were landless peasants and sharecorppers. The Mendoza Project offered to them the prospect of buying their own land over twenty years and access to the newly installed irrigation system. They would be assured of two crops a year instead of the one they harvested at the end of the rainy season. If they lived on the land and pain the annual quota for its purchase, they would receive ownership title to the land.

The irrigation system tapped the mountain springs (*vertientes*) in the nearby mountain range to the south of the river and distributed this water through metal canals on either side of the river. The project was

5

the first serious prospect of new life for the landless "campesinos". The Santa Barbara section of the project included land allotments for about a forty small farms.

The annual cycle of agriculture

In the State of Miranda (ten degrees north of the Equator), the farmers followed the same calendar every year = "slash and burn", sow, cultivate and harvest: ("la tumba", "la siembra". "el repaso" and "la cosecha")

April was the month to slash and burn and May the month to plough the furrows and plant. June and July were the most difficult months and known as "los gemelos" (the twins). These were the months when their supply of corn was low and some seed corn always had to be saved for the next planting. A common expression was "If we can get through "los gemelos", we'll make it through to the harvest in August and September.

It was only after the irrigation project was completed in the late 1930s that a second annual crop could be harvested. Before that, the success of a second crop depended on the arrival of "the latter rains" or "el norte". This crop would be planted in September, with the second harvest coming early the next year.

PART TWO

THE RAMON AND MARIA STORY

AND

THE ANTONIO AND MARY STORY

"The Ramon and Maria Story"

Two peasant families in the Upper Tuy Valley first became linked in friendship and later by marriage because of the meeting of two primary school girls – Petra and Maria - who met at a rural school in Santa Barbara. The year was around 1940.

Beware of *los evangelicos*

Petra: Hola, Maria. Did you know that Father Jose was going up and down the road yesterday telling everyone "Beware of the *evangelicos!* They are dressed like sheep but they are really wolves and trying to sell their books. Since you are one of those people, I thought I should tell you to watch out!

Maria: If the priest is talking about "La Santa Biblia", we have one in our house and my mother reads some verses from that book every day before we leave for school.

Petra: Since I have never even seen one of those books, I guess the priest won't bother me.

Maria: If you would like to see the little book which we call "El Nuevo Testamento", I'll bring you a copy which has the story of Jesus in it.

Petra: Gee, that's nice of you. Yes, I would love to read it since any book that talks about Jesus must be good.

At the city market

Petra and Maria meet up with each other a year later in the public market in Ocumare.

Petra: Maria, long time no see! I haven't seen you since our family moved up to El Chorreron a couple of years ago. You know that we now live a long way back up in the hills and don't get to market very often.

Maria: Yes, I know it is a long way up there. My uncle has a plot of land there and he says it is cooler and the land is better. I remember he told us that there was a brook up there which had a near waterfall where you can take a shower bath. It must be nice to live up there.

Petra: Yes, we are happy in our new home. I now have two little brothers, Miguel and Mario, who are four and six. Believe it or not, we now have a little sister, Nina. She is a darling and will soon be nine. I still have the little book about Jesus you gave me when we were in school together in Santa Barbara.

Maria: I guess you don't see much of Father Jose up there in the hills. I don't think he could ride a mule! He still keeps ranting and raving about how all the *evangelicos* are going to hell. But our little congregation keeps growing and he doesn't bother us much any more. I think he has just written us off as "lost sheep".

Petra: My mother still goes down to the parish church in Ocumare in Holy Week. She loves to hear the stories about Jesus which are in that little book you gave me many years ago. We've had some discussions with the Adventists – another kind of evangelical group. They say that we should keep Saturday not Sunday as a day of rest. We think that they are messed but really do not know enough about the Holy Bible to prove that they are wrong.

Ramon "Suro" and Rafael visit Santa Barbara

Two young country men, aged twenty and twenty-two, appeared at the door of the missionary residence in Santa Barbara on a Sunday afternoon. Since they were to used to knocking on a door to inform you of their presence, they simply shuffled their leather *alpargatas* on the cement steps to announce their arrival. It was just after the hour of the siesta.

Pastor Sinclair: *Buenos dias, pasen adelante. ¿Cómo les puede servir?*

Ramon: Pastor, we are friends of the Espinoza young people who attend your church in Santa Barbara. We have had some long discussions with the Adventists about whether the day of rest should be Saturday or Sunday. We need some help. Our neighbors up in El Chorreron told me that "the true Gospel is taught in the Santa Barbara church and that we should come down here and talk to you.

Pastor Sinclair: Why sure, come in and sit down and we'll visit. It must be boiling hot out there today.

Rafael: Thank you. Frankly we are confused. The Jehovah Witnesses have also been around with their tracts. They sound even more weird than the Adventists. They all confuse us with their line of talk. My parents had all of us kids baptized, but we seldom go to mass. You might say we are not very good Catholics. But my sister has a New Testament so we know some of the stories about Jesus.

Ramón: The Adventists carry a big book – you know, La Santa Biblia, which has a lot more stories than we find in the little book. We think that they call that bigger part – the Old Testament.

(Mrs. Sinclair serves the visitors small cups of thick black coffee and frosted buns and then joins the group in the front room.)

Pastor Sinclair: I suggest you might like to stay for the Bible study this evening when we will talk about the story of the prodigal son. It is moonlight tonight, so you can be on your way back to El Chorreron in the early evening. I know you have to get up early to be in the fields before the sun gets too hot.

Rafael: By the way, pastor, our mother is not well. Someone told us that you have a doctor who comes a couple times a week to your clinic. What are the days when he comes? We can bring our mother down on the burro to see the doctor.

Pastor Sinclair: He comes on Wednesdays and Fridays between seven and nine in the morning. Perhaps you can come down the night before so that you won't miss seeing him. We'll have a place for you to hang your hammocks for the night.

Ramón: Thank you, pastor. Yes, we would like to stay for the evening church meeting. *Que el Señor le bendiga!*

The New Year's gathering

It was six months later when the members of the Lara family attended the annual gathering of the Santa Barbara congregation which they called *La*

Asamblea del Año Nuevo. This tradition began when the early missionaries suggested that this would be one way to break up the raucous, secular activities of the New Year's tradition which came from an old Spanish tradition. The assembly was like a family reunion when they gathered on the day before and the day after New Year's Day. They felt like "a spiritual family" and came together to pray and celebrate the Lord's Supper as they greeted the new year. This tradition was especially meaningful for some members who were from families where only one or two had chosen to join the church. For most of the new believers, this was very important as they bonded with their new "spiritual family".

The afternoon of the last day of the year was celebrated with a huge "sancocho" for which everyone brought something. The meal was a large stew of vegetables, yucca and barbecued goat meat. The veggies and meat were laid out on banana leaves and the juice poured into tin bowels. There was always plenty of food for everyone.

The first day of the year – New Year's Day - was dedicated to sermons and Bible study in the chapel and visiting in the shade of the trees on the mission compound.

Maria: Can somebody help me take this kettle off the fire? It's too heavy for me.

Ramón: I'll be glad to help. Just tell me where to put the kettle.

Maria: Thank you, Ramon. It is good to see you again. How is Mama Blanca and your brother Hipolito?

Ramón: It is thoughtful of you to ask.. Mother is not too well, but she not young any more.

Maria: Stop by the house when you have time. I have some old photos of your sister Petra when she and I went to school together several years ago.

That was the day when Ramón and Maria remembered seeing each other "in a romantic way". He was twenty-two and she was a year younger.

"In the shade of the cuji tree"

There is a traditional folk song with these words. *"Estando yo sentado debajo un cuji, palpito mi corazon acordándome de ti"*. (As I sat under the cuji tree, my heart skipped a beat just thinking about you.)

It was noon and the morning sun was nearing its fiercest heat of the day. Ramón and Hipolito wiped the sweat from their brows as they put down their machetes and collapsed under the old cuji tree for lunch. Ramón had come down from the hills early that day to help get in the last of the bean crop before the rainy season began.

Maria appeared with the noon lunch – *arepas con fijoles y queso blanco* – served on a table cloth spread on the ground.

Ramón: Hi, Maria, you brought the *pocho* just in time. I am famished!

Maria: It is a pleasant surprise to see you here. I thought that your brother was coming down to help Hipolito today.

Ramón: He had some other work he promised to do for a neighbor, so I said I would come down and take his place.

Hipólito came along just then and asked to be excused for a few minutes to move the donkeys over to graze in another part of the hillside.

Maria sat down in the shade of the cuji tree. Ramon joined her, fanning his face with his straw sombrero.

Maria: Suro, I hope you don't mind if I call you "Suro" and not Ramon.

Ramón: That's alright. Since my dad's name is also Ramon, the family keeps us straight by calling me by my nickname "Suro". Maria, you are a sight for sore eyes. How nice to see you again.

Maria: Now I have two friends in the Lara family – Petra and you. You know that we have some relatives over in El Siquiri where she is teaching now. I can tell you about some of them since you'll be meeting them at next year's New Year gathering here in Santa Barbara.

Ramon: That's great. I'll stop by after work before I head back up the trail.

(Later in the early evening in the patio of the Espinoza house. The sun was setting and the sliver of a new moon has just appeared on the horizon.)

Maria: Well, Suro, there are a lot of Espinoza relatives over in Siquiri. You will like them – of course, some more than others, to be sure.

Ramon: Maria, I really want to talk about you and me, not the relatives. You are a very special new friend. You have come into my life so suddenly. I really can't tell you how nice it is to get to know you.

Maria: Suro, those are very pleasant words. Frankly I have been thinking about how good it is to know someone like you.

The conversation continued until the shades of night settled in and they both had to bid each other a reluctant good night.

Maria: Bye, Suro, my special friend. I'll see you next Sunday.

Ramon: Maria, goodbye. I won't be seeing you any too soon!

The class for new church members

As the weeks and months went by, Ramon and Maria spent more and more time together. He attended the class for new members which was often attended by members of the church who came to listen. Maria had been a church member since a teenager but attended. The class met late Sunday afternoon in the patio of the Espinoza home since the tin roof of the church building made it very hot in the later afternoon.

There were six persons in the class: Suro, his brother Rafael, a new couple who had attended a Pentecostal church before moving to Santa Barbara, an aged grandmother who had come to live with her daughter and a local school teacher who was *un simpatizante* ("a seeker") who had not yet made up his mind about church memberhiiip and had questions for the pastor.

Pastor Sinclair was always asked questions: How did the Protestant church get started? What was the Reformation? Why do priests not marry? Why do we not have the seven sacraments like the Roman Catholics? What about the Orthodox Christians, the religion of the Greek merchants in Ocumare? They seemed to like to come to our church and sing hymns which they had never heard in their churches. Of course there were discussions about the beliefs of the Adventists and the Jehovah Witnesses. And to be sure, there were questions about the Second Coming of Jesus and the Final Judgment.

The proposal

It was one sultry afternoon after the new member class that Ramón and Maria were sitting in a hammock under the old cuji tree. It was the hour before the evening worship service. Maria brought out from the house a jug of papaya juice which she had chilled in the water pool at the spring.

Ramón: I have been waiting to say something to you for a long time. You and I are not getting any younger. I think that it is time I settled down, you know get married and raise a family.

Maria: Yes, I have been having some of the same thoughts. I really don't want to be an old maid. I would like to settle down, too.

Ramón: Well that makes two of us that need to make a decision pretty soon. Maria, will you marry me? That's the question I have been wanting to ask you for a long time.

Maria: That's so sudden, but I confess that I have been hoping that you would ask me. I would rather be with you than anyone I have ever known.

Ramón: (Putting his arm around her, stroking her hand and then kissing her neck) I could never be happy with anyone but you.

Maria: I would be honored to become your wife. I know that you would make me very, very happy.

The two lovers embraced each other with passion and pressed their bodies together.

Ramón: Don't you think I should ask your mother and brother for permission to take you to be my wife.? You know I am building a new hut on my plot of land and will soon be harvesting the corn and bean crops. I am also fattening a pig so we could have a barbeque at our wedding.

The wedding

Pastor Sinclair officiated at their wedding on a late Sunday afternoon in the Santa Barbara chapel. They had been married in a civil marriage service by the local judge in Ocumare the day before. The family and friends were gathering for the evening service so the sanctuary was filled to overflowing.

Ramón wore a *"liqui liqui"* suit with a high collar. It was made by the local tailor from several yards of white linen. Maria wore a simple white dress with a lace vest which she had borrowed from her sister-in-law. A local taxi was hired to drive the couple from the chapel to the foot of the trail six miles away. From there they walked the final three miles on the trail which lead to their home in El Chorreron.

According to the pastoral records of Pastor Sinclair, the wedding was celebrated on December 2, 1955.

Their first home

The hut was made of *bajareque* (adobe bricks) with a roof made of sheets of tin, with gutters to catch the rain water in a fifty gallon oil drum. The floor was of tamped earth with a layer of clay laid over to settle the dust. There was a door with a leather "latch string" connected to a wooden 'catch". The only window was covered with two paneled wooden shutters.

The "kitchen" was at the side of the house under a sheltered wing of the hut. An adobe brick table served for cooking with a wood or charcoal fire for cooking and boiling water. Bags of corn, yucca and dried onions were hung nearby and there was "la vieja" – a post with a wooden "boca" served to squeeze the sugar cane juice to sweeten the coffee. "Un pilon" to grind the corn was nearby.

In the patio was always a flock of chickens. A goat was tethered nearby which provided their daily milk. At a short distance was the pig pen for the sow and her piglets. Animals and chickens took care of the disposal of the refuse from the kitchen.

"El excusado" (a pit toilet) was located some twenty yards from the hut. Ramon had put in an application at the local sanitation office for a government cement pit toilet.

Their furniture was simple: a bed made from a tanned ox hide, two homemade wooden chairs and a table. There were two small trunks for personal belonging and papers. Clothes were hung on wooden pegs on the plastered mud walls.

This humble dwelling was "their own home" !

The birth of Nehemias Ramon Lara Espinoza

Maria spent the last month of her pregnancy with her mother, Mama Blanca, at the family home in Santa Barbara. Her brother, Hipolito, and his wife, Rosalia, and their children lived on the next plot of land.

The baby was delivered by Mama Blanca, the village midwife and Maria's mother. A packet of sterile gauze and medications were purchased at the local drug store. Ramon and a friend sat patiently outside and then were invited in to see the new baby. Mama Blanca proudly lifted her newest grandson, a two kilo, six ounce baby and placed him in the arms of the new father. The baby had good lungs and a huge appetite.

The baby's name – if a son – had been chosen ahead of time. He would be called Nehemias. The pastor had just finished a series of sermons on that Biblical hero The new parents had agreed on the name and trusted that the baby would grow up to have the courage, wisdom and compassion of their hero in the Bible story.

Two days later, Ramon went to the register's office in Ocumare to record the name of his son: Nehemias Ramon Lara Espinoza.

Ramon, a commissioned lay pastor

He was a born leader, preacher and pastor. After he had become a church member, he studied a lay training course with the local pastor and then enrolled in a correspondence course with the radio station "Voz de Los

Andes" in Quito, Ecuador. Over a period of nearly sixty years he served as a lay pastor in several congregations. He was recognized n 2009 as "pastor emeritus" by the *Iglesia Evangélica Presbiteriana de Venezuela*

In the pictorial section of this book is a photograph of him preaching in the Santa Barbara church. It was taken in the month of a special evangelistic emphasis with the theme *"Cristo nos librará"*. This photo shows the first modifications in the mud walled chapel. Two windows had been opened behind the pulpit. The worshippers could then see the sky and the trees which marked the boundary of the land on which the chapel stood. The chapel had been the home of the Espinoza family, built in the 1930s and given to the congregation in the late 1940s.

The sermon that Ramón preached that day may well have been something like the following:

"The Session of our congregation has chosen this text which tells us the most important part of the "Good News of Jesus Christ":

-   Christ frees us from our sinful past – whatever that may be for each of us: a life of greed, envy or whatever;

-   Christ frees us to live a new life – a better life – a life filled with love, faith and hope.

We do not know what the future will bring. But we are sure that if we take our responsibility as Christians, that we will have a better community for us and our neighbors. Remember that Jesus taught us to love our neighbors as we love ourselves. So I invite you to join in singing a simple but very important hymn:

"Librará, librará, Cristo nos librará".

A few years later – a turning point in the congregation

During the 1960s, the congregation did not have a resident ordained pastor. Some of the members had "fallen away" and others had moved away. The services were held only when a visiting pastor came along. It seemed that the congregation was dying.

However Ramon felt a call to bring the people together and talk about the future of their congregation. According to the story, he started to ring the church bell, ringing it for a long time, until a crowd gathered at the church. Some thought that there had been an accident or some important news to be shared with the neighborhood.

Ramon simply stood before those who showed up and announced:

"Since we do not have a pastor, I feel that God has called me to be your pastor. I know that I am just a lay pastor, but I am willing to be your leader and help you revive our congregation. Are you with me?"

It was clear that he deserved to be their leader. He was respected and loved by the community and that God had called him to lead them as their pastor. The rest of the story unfolded as the Presbytery acted to commission him as pastor of the congregation, to serve the Lord's Supper and to represent the congregation at the meetings of the presbytery.

As the congregation looks back over the years, Ramon's initiative to ring the church bell and call the congregation back to worship, was the way that God was working to revive God's work in Santa Barbara.

AN AFTERWORD

As of the writing of this story in 2012, Ramon is still with us, even though Maria was called to Her Heavenly Reward more than five years ago. As he lives out the remainder of his twilight years, his family and friends give thanks to God for these two dedicated lives. They have left to their extended family and the community a treasure of enduring value far beyond any human estimate.

ANTONIO AND MARY: a missionary nurse and a Venezuelan artist.

The author celebrated the marriage of Antonio Rivero and Mary Janice Armbruster on June 5, 1954 in "El Redentor" Presbyterian Church, Caracas, Venezuela. He shared in this ceremony with the Reverend Alfonso Lloreda, pastor of the congregation.

Much of their story is recorded in a taped interview by Mary Rivero in 1982. This tape and translation is in the personal library of the author.

Mary

Mary, born in 1922, was reared on a family farm in Ohio and graduated valedictorian from the Nevada High School. She attended Presbyterian youth conferences at the College of Wooster. Early in her life she felt called to be "a missionary nurse" and graduated from the White Cross Hospital Nursing School in Columbus. She then spent a year in specialized training in midwifery with the Frontier Nursing Service in Kentucky.

After language and orientation school in Medellin, Colombia in 1945 she was assigned to Casa Sion, a community center in a lower-middle class neighborhood of "old Caracas". There she staffed a day care clinic and did home visitation. During that time she met a young Venezuelan artist, Antonio Rivero, when they both sang in the choir of El Redentor Presbyterian Church. Antonio was to become her husband eight years later.

After serving at Casa Sion, she was assigned to begin a medical ministry in the Centro Cristiano Rural in Santa Barbara del Tuy with the Reverend and Mrs. C. Paul Russell. This was a ministry to rural families who had settled on land grants in the Mendoza Rural Colony in the 1930s. She was assisted in this pioneer ministry by volunteer doctors in the district seat of Ocumare, seven miles away. Mary was trusted and beloved by those she served in their homes at all hours of the day and night.

After her marriage to Antonio in 1954 and their move to the United States in 1958, she changed vocations and became a teacher of high school Spanish. This afforded her the opportunity to work and still be available to the family. In later years she returned to do graduate work and received a M.A. in counseling from Miami University. In the early 1970s the family moved to Tampa, Florida where she enjoyed volunteering at the St. John Presbyterian Church, a bi-lingual congregation. There she was elected a ruling elder.

She and Antonio are the proud parents of their seven children, eleven grandchildren, and twenty great grandchildren. (Note: Six children of Antonio were from his first marriage. The seventh child was from his marriage to Mary). She died at the age of eighty-six in 2008. Mary will be remembered as a wonderful wife and mother, a devoted missionary nurse and teacher. She was truly "a light in the world" and an advocate for the sick and the poor.

Antonio

Antonio was born in 1919 in the remote backlands of the Tuy Valley near Santa Teresa. The area bordered the Rio Siquiri which emptied into the Tuy River. Antonio remembered riding on a donkey as a little boy in company with his mother and older sisters to attend an Evangelical service led by students from a Bible institute.

His father died when he was small and he remembered little about him. His widowed mother, Señora Rosario, a rural school teacher, was a strong and determined woman. She embraced wholeheartedly the Evangelical faith and gathered her brood and set out for Caracas. There she wanted to find an Presbyterian church and education for her children in the mission primary school. She also did not want her four attractive daughters to be caught in the web of the common law marriage of the rural culture.

Señora Rosario's only "bank account" was a few cows since she supplemented her meager teacher's salary by buying and selling cows. She decided to sell one cow and leave the others with a neighbor to keep. With that money she set off for Caracas where she had an uncle who had promised to help her. Senora Rosario had been born and reared in Caracas and so never felt comfortable in the rural area where she had married and taught school.

Through contacts with the Presbyterian missionaries she was given work as "a Bible woman". These humble women visited in homes and distributed Christian literature in the poor barrios of Caracas. These church visitors were received in homes in ways that no pastor could be received. Señora

Rosario was a brave and competent Christian evangelist. Her children found in her a model of faith and fortitude. As a boy, Antonio earned some money by carrying large cans of water from a public fountain to homes which did not have city water service. This cash helped in the family's meager budget.

The most significant result of their new life in Caracas was to receive scholarships to attend the Colegio Americano, a mission school founded in 1895. Antonio would arise at five to carry water "to his clients" and arrived at school by eight. At the Colegio Americano he came under the benevolent influence of Miss Dorothy Parnell and Miss Verna Phillips. Early they recognized his gifts as a student and also his lovely tenor voice.

The family soon found a church home at El Redentor Presbyterian Church as well as an education for their children in the Colegio Americano which was near the church. Antonio always considered that it was the Providence of God which permitted him to receive a good primary education at the mission school. He spoke often of the influence of the American missionary and national teachers in his life. He became a church member as a teenager. For a few years he sang in the choir at the Roman Catholic cathedral under the direction of Professor Pedro R. Gutierrez, the celebrated composer of Venezuela's most beloved son, "Alma llanera".

By the time Antonio was in his late teens, a newly arrived missionary, the Reverend Bancroft Reifsnyder challenged the youth of El Redentor Church with "a more progressive understanding of the Gospel". He led them to see that God was calling them to become involved in the future of their nation, as well as in the development of their personal faith.

It was also in the mid 1940s that Mr. Clair Johnson was sent by the South American YMCA (called in Spanish: *ACJ – Asociacion Cristiana de Jovenes*) to establish programs in the barrios of Caracas. Antonio was one of the first sixteen members of the Caracas branch of the YMCA
Antonio was a barber and supplemented his meager income by selling his art. He had only a short course in painting, but possessed native ability as an artist. He married Josephina when he was nineteen and they had six children. As the years went by, their marriage unraveled and Antonio found

himself a single parent with six children between the ages of four and fourteen.

It was during those years that he fell in love with Mary Armbruster, a missionary nurse. She was thirty- two when they were married in 1954. Antonio found work as a commercial art designer. He developed his English which he learned at the Colegio Americano. He greatly improved the command of English during a three month tour in the United States with a church singing group which visited the States in 1952.

The family and the resistance movement

After the brief three-year dawn of democracy in 1945 under the *Acción Democrática* , there was a military coup in 1948. A "*junta*" of generals ruled Venezuela with an iron fist. The *Acción Democrática* party immediately began to function underground during the years of the military dictatorship. Even though traditionally the Evangelicals (read "Protestants") were not involved in politics in Venezuela, this brutal dictatorship spawned a clandestine movement in which several Evangelicals men and women played important roles.

Antonio's family and other members of *El Redentor* Church were involved in the underground movement. An important book containing names, addresses and code words was secretly hidden in a wall of the Rivero home. The secret police were aware that such a book existed but could not discover where it was kept.

The code word for the resistance movement and its records was "los muchachitos" or "the little children". Antonio and Mary had rented their home to a relative when they moved after their marriage to live and work in Ocumare del Tuy at the Centro Cristiano Rural. Since Mary was an American citizen she would be less a suspect involved in the resistance movement. She would periodically stop by the family home in Caracas to inquire "*?Cómo están los muchachitos?*" to be sure that "the book" had not been discovered. The answer was always "*Si, señora, los muchachitos están bien de salud y muy contentos!*".

However the secret police arrested two neighbors, Señoras Carmen Veitia and Carmen Crillo and were tortured. Señora Veitia was an active member of *El Redentor* Church,   Later when democracy triumphed she became the secretary of the wife of the President and was honored on several occasions for her work with the resistance movement. The President of the Republic sent a floral offering to the funeral service of Senora Rosario Rivero, Antonio's mother. A family member said this about her:: "If Señora Rosario had seen such a "corona" of flowers, she would have laughed and said that she did not deserve such an honor". The names of several of the Rivero family and relatives appear in the literature about the resistance movement of the 1950s.

During those difficult years, Antonio was concerned that his family was being watched and might be arrested by the secret police. He even experienced a slight nervous breakdown and was hospitalized for a short time. It was then that he shared with Mary (who had been kept out of the information chain) how deeply the Rivero family was involved in the clandestine movement. Antonio then advised Mary "If the police arrest me, you are to take the children and go to the American Embassy". Antonio wanted to be sure to protect his children and their American mother by seeking "political asylum" if necessary.

The family moves to the United States

In the 1958, Antonio, now an experienced graphic designer, felt that he could find work in the United States. With Mary's connection in her home state of Ohio they could locate the family permanently there. He found a job near Dayton and the family bought a home in Trenton, Ohio. The move proved a blessing for them and their children. The Reverend Robert E. Lodwick, a former missionary in Brazil, was their pastor and friend during those transitional years.

As the years went by, the author and his wife have visited the Rivero family on several occasions in their retirement home in Tampa, Florida. Our family deeply values this life-long friendship. The family was saddened by Mary's death in 2008 at the age of 86. Antonio, now 93. lives out his life "in the slow lane", cared for lovingly by his son Eli in Tampa, Florida. The extended family is scattered over several states, but keep in close touch with each other.

PART THREE

Vignettes of their neighbors

A note about the vignettes

The author has chosen these brief "pen portraits" from the different groups of inhabitants of the Upper Tuy Valley. The majority were landless peasants whose forebears were indigenous, African, Iberian, European and Anglo Saxon.

These "neighbors" were dirt farmers, day laborers, merchants, military and public officials, each carrying a unique story. Together, they provide "a collage" of the rural society of the 1950.

THE GREEK CLOTH MERCHANTS

Among the locals with whom Suro and Maria's life was cast were two families of Greek immigrant merchants. Venezuela was opening to European immigrants who soon found jobs in the expanding economy. "The traveling salesman", know as "un marchante" (a person who sells from door to door calling out his wares) was a common figure in a peasant society.

"El griego" (Sergio Papazitkos) and "el otro griego" (Demos Karios) stood out in the crowded market plaza. They were noticed not only because of their foreign accent, but also because of their lighter skin color. Above all they were aggressive merchants and always managing to sell just below the prices offered by the native sellers. Only the immigrant Italian butcher was in their same category in the village.

Cloth was an imported basic commodity in the early days, since the native cotton industry was still in its infancy. The "marchante" traveled, not only from door to door, but from market to market, in his small "carry all" truck, It was loaded with bolts of cloth, sheets of buttons and snaps and boxes of sandals, caps and straw hats: all protected from the sun and rain by an old green tarp.

The Greeks bought their goods from a large Greek-owned importer in Caracas which enabled them to undersell the local merchants. They were prospering!

The two families

Sergio's wife, Suhela, was a beautiful woman in her early twenties. She would tend the store while Sergio was out on the road selling. They lived in a couple of rooms behind the rented store building.. Demos, his business partner, had not brought his wife from Greece, so he lived in a room in a local boarding house.

Since the only other foreigners in town were "los Americanos" in Santa Barbara (just five miles away), it was natural that they would seek them out. Sergio was of the Greek Evangelical Church, rather different among the Greeks who were usually of the Greek Orthodox faith. He had come from the small city of Berea in Macedonia which is mentioned in the Bible (Acts: 17-:10. This is the modern city of Verria). He knew his Bible and wanted to find others to share his faith. His wife and Demos came along with him to visit the church "of the Americanos" in Santa Barbara.

They joined the congregation for worship from time to time and added "an international dimension" to the small Protestant congregation of native Venezuelans"

The affair with the Italian butcher

Since Sergio was out on the road often while Suhela minded the store, the Italian butcher (whose shop was close by) came as often as possible to bring the daily meat order to Sergio's home. He seemed to overstay his visits long enough to cause "the tongues to wag" and the gossip to circulate "there's something going on between the butcher and the attractive Greek lady". This was not a pleasant situation which would easily blow over. (Note: Years late the author visited them in Verria, Greece to find Sergio and Suhela, divorced and both remarried.)

ANTONIO ORTEGA, THE PEDDLER

He was an important member of the community and church. He was married to a lovely, but sickly, younger woman, Isabel, with whom he reared three children, Manases, Metabel and Deborah. The family lived directly across the road from "El Buen Pastor" Church in Santa Barbara.

Antonio was "a businessman" or more precisely, a traveling salesman. In the local parlance he was known as "un quincallero", a dealer in "baratajas" (small objects of little value). His wares were packed in a suitcase: nails, screws, staples, bolts, nuts, washers, soap, lotions and "you – name –it". His place of business was any place where there were potential customers. Antonio was a bright man who made a good impression. And he always carried a few portions of the Scriptures and a New Testament for sale.

His wife, Isabel, was a capable woman, but quite frail. She was an avid reader and thoughtful wife and mother. She loved her Bible and drew daily from that well of inspiration for herself, her family and neighbors. When she was not well, Antonio would fetch the daily supply of water from the village well. He would stand in line with the women at the well, take his turn filling his five gallon lard can, hoist in on his shoulder and walk up the road with the other women. Few husbands would stoop to do "women's work".

Two of their three children turned out well. Manases became a successful school teacher and Deborah married the manager of the local radio station. They moved up from poverty to a lower middle class life. All we remember of Metabal is that the neighbors just said : "she went off to Caracas"!

Antonio, one of the "encargados"

Under the leadership of Pastor Lee who was burdened with the responsibility of a second congregation, a group of volunteer lay preachers was prepared. A lay leadership training course was offered which Antonio successfully completed. "Los encargados" would take turns leading the Wednesday Bible studies at the church, as well as lead "house meetings" in nearby neighborhoods. On several occasion, an evening service was held near the local "bolas court" where men gathered in the evening to play the popular Venezuelan version of bowling. An electric generator and projector, mounted on the Jeep, would present colored filmstrips and moving pictures in the early evenings. Manasés operated the projector and Antonio closed every showing with a brief spiritual thought.

A story from one of the Bible study sessions reflect the challenges the lay preachers had in their ministry since they had only studied a brief lay training course. On one occasion, the Bible study was from a writing of St. Paul in which there was a reference to "licentious women". Antonio had misread "the licentious" as "the licensed" women. The group tried to figure out why Paul was against the women who were licensed. Felix Aleman (a rather well educated member) observed "I think we are in error. The Apostle was talking about the licentious, not the licensed". Then the Bible study got back on track!

As in the times of the Apostle Paul, when the Gospel was scattered along the Roman roads by travelers: peddlers, soldiers, converted soothsayers and others who shared the Good News of Jesus where ever they went. Antonio Ortega, was a part of that illustrious number of believers in Jesus who spread the Gospel wherever they traveled.

A TALENTED YOUNG MAN GOES TO CARACAS

Juan was the next to the youngest of the Espinoza family. He was both bright and personable. On several occasions he spent time in Caracas with his eldest brother, Graciliano, an elder in the Sion Presbyterian Church. The church was located in a worker barrio, La Pastora, named for the historic church in that part of the old city.

This barrio had been chosen by the new social agency Asociación Cristiana de Jóvenes (YMCA in Venezuela) for one of its first neighborhood athletic programs. Casa Sion stood beside the small church, with a day clinic and an apartment for a missionary nurse. The vacant lot behind the chapel was cleared by a group of volunteers and made into a volley ball court with a shower and toilet. It was a great success even though the parish priest objected openly to "the Protestant invasion". The ACJ was dubbed by most Catholics as a Protestant organization.

Juan was interested in trying his limited English with the ACJ Director, Claire Johnson. There were volunteer coaches drawn from the Union Church, the interdenominational congregation of English-speaking Americans and Europeans. There was a "Y's Men Club" which included some members of El Redentor Presbyterian Church downtown.

Juan wanted to find a job and live in the big city. He was employed by the ACJ as a clerk in their office downtown where their sports programs and social events were coordinated. It was just the right job for Juan and he could live in the home of his brother's family.

However, he did not remain in Caracas for more than a few months. He just did not have the skills needed to hold the position. After a probation period on the job, he did not get a permanent job. So he went back to Santa Barbara, yes, discouraged but ready to try something else. He was twenty years old.

Juan, the medical assistant and adult education teacher

The missionary nurse in Santa Barbara needed an assistant, since the medical program was expanding. Mary asked Juan if he would like to learn to give injections and do home visitation to lighten her work load. He responded with enthusiasm. The medical practice in rural areas was to use injections for most medicines since patients were careless about taking them according to the prescription instructions. Also because of the lack of clocks and watches in most households, patients did not take their medications on schedule.

Juan also became the teacher of the adult literacy classes in Santa Barbara and Siquiri. Since the sun rises and sets at about the same hour the year around near the Equator, the classes began an hour after sunset. There were usually five or six young men who showed up. The Laubach literacy materials were invaluable and Juan was a good teacher. A photo in the picture section of this book shows him constructing rustic tables for the class, with two boys looking on who probably should have been attending the local primary school! In that photo one sees the rustic shelter, called *"una tinglada"* with a heavy wire fence to keep the chickens, pigs and donkeys out of the class room!

The adult literacy program lasted for only a few years in, but it was one of Juan's lasting contributions to these rural communities.

His marriage to Nina Lara

Shortly after returning from Caracas, he met Nina Lara, a sister of Ramon Lara. Nina was not only bright and confident, but a good organizer. It was not long before Juan and Nina were married, much to the delight of both their families. An additional room was built on the Espinoza family home for the newly weds who were married in a simple ceremony in the Santa Barbara Church in 1961. He was twenty-six and she nineteen.

Juan had learned to drive the mission station wagon. He would often transport patients to the emergency room in the district hospital in Ocumare. He was ennamored with the power of the vehicle and the prestige of being able to drive. He was not a good driver and had a fatal accident at an intersection on the main road from Santa Barbara to Ocumare. He was only 27 and left a sad young widow of twenty-one.

TWO LONESOME MEN

Román, the town barber

No one really knew where he came from or his real family name. He just
appeared from nowhere one day and "moved in" to the spare room behind
the church meeting room in the former Espinoza family home. He said that
"the Lord had sent him there in a vision to testify for Jesus". He possessed
on old Bible, a hammock and some barber tools. He seemed to have only
one pair of pants and a faded jacket.

He made a low table with adobe bricks for his small kerosene stove, found a
old chair and a white cloth and was "open for business". He charged only
one bolivar (US$.0.33) for a haircut and shave.

No one tried to dislodge him from the church building, since he would
always quote the words of San Pablo "I can not be disobedient to the
heavenly vision". The customer would endure his sermons about Jesus and
the need for salvation. This invitation was often given when the razor was at
the customer's throat!

Román had only one good eye. The other eye seemed to wander. He said it
was his "bad eye", but some thought it was really a glass eye.

As the years went by, the old church building had to be torn down so that the
new cement block church could be erected on the site. What could the
congregation do with Roman? The mission had a piece of land near the
highway which would be ideal for a small shack for Román. "A work day"
was set and lumber and roofing was assembled. Román's house was erected
in a few hours. Since another village barber had arrived and took away his
only source of income, Román was given a simple job of watering the plants
and trees around the pastor's residence. This he did faithfully - but always
he watered at "the hour of the siesta" (1 – 3 p.m.) which bothered the pastor
who took his siesta at the same hour. He argued with Román that it was not
good for the plants to be watered during the hottest hours of the day, but it
was to no available. Román was determined to water the plants at trees at the
hour which he felt was right!

What ever happened to Román? He became a public problem as his mental
health degenerated and his health was severely impaired. He also claimed he

had another "heavenly vision" which was that the Lord had told him to marry one of the young girls in the congregation! Thanks to the local public health officer, a place was found for him in the state mental hospital to which he was transferred. The guise of moving him was that he was going to live in a place where he would have indoor plumbing and running water in his room. This convinced him to follow the doctor's orders for once!

But how can we every forget the one-eyed barber with the "heavenly vision"!

Bernardino, another man who came from nowhere

He was not like Román. He had no heavenly vision and no strong opinions. He was sweet natured and always wore a smile. He seems to have no "oficio" (vocation or profession). He was happy to be a day laborer and was satisfied with whatever the patron paid him. He had found an abandoned hut, with a leaky roof ,and just "moved in". Some neighbors gave him a can of asphalt tar to stop the leaks in the tin roof. He had an old water barrel to catch the roof water and a :privy" on the lot from the previous occupant.

Bernardino always came to church. He would arrive late and sit on a back bench. He stood for the hymns, but didn't sing. He always left before the offering was taken towards the close of the service. Everyone knew Bernardino and smiled back at his broad, childish grin.

One Sunday he did not appear at church. An elder offered to go down to check on him. The report was that he found him stretched on the floor, groaning and holding his hands on his stomach. Together the elders hired the local taxi and took him to the hospital in Ocumare.

His condition was serious – an advanced cancer which was inoperable. The doctor gave him just a few days to live. Members of the church took turns sitting with him until he expired late one evening. Since burials had to be completed within twenty-four hours, the elders agreed to take a collection among the church members to buy his coffin and see that he had a decent burial. The cheapest wooden coffin was 50 bolivars or about $US16.00. A simple wooden cross with the name "Bernardino. un hijo de Dios" was prepared.

Pastor Sinclair and the elders carried the rough coffin from the pickup truck to the open grave site just as the sun was setting behind the western hills. Before the body was lowered into the grave, this prayer was offered:

"Dear God, We commend to you of dear friend Bernardino. We know only his first name, and do not know when he was born. But you, O Loving Father, know his last name and when he was born. Take care of our friend, Bernardino, He was a good man and never hurt any one. Peace be with him. Amen"

THE MILITARY, THE POWER ELITE AND THE COLONISTS

ILLEGAL LAND OCCUPANCY

The established regulations of the Mendoza colonization project stated that each "colono" who was granted a plot of land must live on the property and cultivate the land The author has chosen three situations which may have occurred in the colony and come to the District Court in the 1950s for resolution. The names of the complainents which are used are intended to protect their possible identity.

CASE: Federal Colonia Mendoza vs. Lt. Pablo Ramirez Soto

The lawyer of the Mendoza Colony attested that the occupant of the land was Fidel Belisario, an employee of Lt. Pablo Ramirez Soto who held title to the land. Sr. Belisario was paid a salary by Lt. Ramirez to whom he turned over the entire crop grown on the land. Lt. Ramirez did not live on the land or cultivate it.

The court awarded the land to Sr. Belisario as the legitmate owner and ordered that Lt. Ramirez pay $2,500 bolivares for each year that he did not live on the land year to Sr. Belisario for the loss of the value of the crops since he began to work for said person.

FALSIFICATION OF WEIGHTS AND MEASURES

CASE: Federal Colonia Mendoza vs. Sr. Mario Sabanes V., owner of "Bodega, La Fortuna" of Santa Barbara del Tuy.

The lawyer of the Federal government testified that this shop owner had deliberately bribed the District Inspector of Weights and Measurements to certify a set of weights and measures which did not conform to government standards. The evidence produced in court showed that the weights were at least 30% less than the officially certified weights.

The court ordered that the said inspector be fired without right to severance pay and pension benefits and that Sr. Sabanes be imprisoned for one year which is a stated in the Law # 394 which penalizes anyone who makes or uses uncertified or false weights and measures.

(Note: The judge after he had pronounced the sentence, added these words:

"I would like to remind Sr. Sabanes that he has also broken the law of God because the Prophet Micah (Micah 6:11) said "The Lord does not tolerate wicked scales or a bag of dishonest weights".

SEXUAL ABUSE OF A FEMALE EMPLOYEE

CASE :   Sr. Nicodemes Paredes Serrano vs. Sr. Rogelio Garcia Valentín related to the sexual abuse of an employee, brought against Sr. Paredes by the father of Domitila Garcia Mendoza, minor of 17 years age.

The court appointed a defense lawyer since Sr. Garcia claimed poverty as the reason he could not employee a lawyer.

The witnesses brought to the court were: Dr. Pedro Espinoza, public health officer and part-time obstetrician at the Ocumare District Hospital and Srta. Migdalia Moreno, an employee of Sr.Paredes. Dr. Espinoza affirmed that a male child was born to Srta. Garcia at the District Hospital and is presently being cared for in the hospital nursery.. Srta. Garcia told the court that Sr. Paredes had on several occasions forced her into his bedroom and raped her. Srta. Moreno confirmed that her roommate, Srta. Garcia, had told her repeatedly of these assaults. Srta. Martinez told the court that Sr. Paredes had said that if she told anyone of these assaults that she would not only be fired, but that he would inform her father that he was already preparing to fire her because she had stolen some household items..

The court decreed that Sr. Paredes should pay child support for the male child of $500 bolivares per month until he reached six years of age. If Sr. Paredes is delinquent in the payment of child support that a lien will be placed against his property for that amount until the full child support is paid.

(Note: This case is probably the exception in the Ocumare District. Most cases of this nature did not arrive at the court for adjudication.]

THE SECRET CELL OF THE RESISTANCE

Not only were the primary school teachers angry with the decree of the military junta to dissolve their union, but the military was also stealing land in the Colony.

The term "milicos", a pejorative term which translated meant "the big boys" or "the army guys", was often used by the people. Instead of protecting the people as they had sworn to do in their oath of allegiance, they often seemed to be the enemies of the people.

How did all this happen so quickly? The military had simply adopted a strategy to plant "orejas" or "spies" in the farm community and at the same time steal land which could have been occupied by needy landless peasants.

How did they do it? It was easy for those in power. Lieut. Ponce just had a peasant in his employ live on the land, was paid a salary by the officer, but turned over the produce of his plot to "the boss" who pocketed the profit. But the most important part of the strategy was that the occupant of the land became one of the "orejas" who reported to the boss on any person or event in the village which might be a threat to the military government.

The planting of the bomb in the military jeep

It was at a meeting of the "Cell XXI"' under the cuji tree on the school grounds after the students had gone home that Maestro Granados told the small group that he had been taken to the military post, questioned and kept overnight. The accusation (received from "una oreja") was that he had been distributing "folletos" (tracts) at the village story which were political in nature. The judge did not have any material evidence, but warned the teacher to be careful about the papers he distributed.

Senor Granados said that he had told the judge that he had passed out some copies of the Gospel of John. He was an Evangelical and wanted his friends to read the words of Jesus.

The next week one of the teachers who was a cell member was taken in to the police for questioning because it was reported that he had said derogatory words about the local military commander. The cell members felt it was time to show "los milicos" that they should lay off the local people. Some suggested that they knew how to get a "car bomb" which was a simple explosive device, which was attached to the ignition switch. It would detonate the bomb when the ignition was turned on. It only had the power to disable the motor and perhaps cause the windshield to shatter. It wasn't 'a big bomb", but it would scare the "milicos" and let them know that the local people were upset.

Heraclio; You all know that kid named "Miqueas". We could get him to place the car bomb in the jeep at the military post when the soldier takes a break to go to the store or to the outhouse to relieve himself. That kid is smart. We can give him a few *bolivares* to do the job. He doesn't like the "milico" anyway because he is always threatening to take him to jail if he doesn't stop skipping school.

Eladio: Let's do it and see what happens.

PART FOUR

The Santa Barbara congregation

and

The Christian Rural Center

THE GOSPEL MESSAGE IN RURAL VENEZUELA EN 1950s

What did the Gospel message mean to country people in rural Venezuela , subjected to the miserable economic and political conditions and controlled by a greedy military cast?

Certainly there was the consoling message of personal salvation. God cared about each one of them. God was ready to receive the sincere believer and bless that person with God's love and mercy. But what else?

The "exodus story" came alive for them. Venezuela was like Egypt where economic, political and military powers kept the Israelites in virtual bondage. They wanted to be free. They knew the story of "The Promised Land" and God's promise that God would give them that place of security and hope.

Yet they knew that between them and freedom there was a body of water (The Red Sea) and a desert (The Sinai Wilderness". The questions were: how could they escape, cross that sea and survive in that wilderness?

The exodus story makes sense to any oppressed people. The present-day "sons of Jacob" have found a new faith which assures them that God cares about them. This "good news" made sense to the rural families of Santa Barbara. Yes, we can be freed, we can get across that sea and through that wilderness. Yes, we can get to the Promised Land!

Their new found faith melded with their dream of political and social liberation. It was with this understanding of the Gospel that the story of FAITH AND FREEDOM unfolded in the 1950s in the Tuy Valley.

FAMILIES OF THE SANTA BARBARA CONGREGATIONS

Juan and Blanca Espinoza
  Graciliano, Hipolito, Juan, Domingo, Maria and an older daughter

Ramon and Catalina Lara
  Nelson, Ramon Antonio, Rafael, Luis, Mario, Miguel, Cipriano, Nina and Petra

Salome and Suzana Martinez
  Domital, Emma and two sons

The Felix Aleman family

The Rivero family

The Moline family

The Geronimo Serrano family

The Eladio and Dorotea Orasma family

The Echenique family

The Estansilao Rondon family

LA IGLESIA PRESBTERIANA 'EL BUEN PASTOR" - Santa Barbara

The beginnings of the congregation

Around 1923, an evangelist Manuel Key, took up residence in Paracotos, an isolated village about fifteen miles (by mule trail) from the capital city of the State of Miranda, Los Teques.

Paracotos was one of the most remote villages in the state with no road connection to the outside world. There was a proverb among the rural people: "Ni se sabe en Paracotos" ("Not even in Paracotos it is known"!) The mule trails were used for the transportation of the beans, corn and coffee produced in the region. The Paracotos River (really a stream) gave the area much fertile soil and cool uplands to grow coffee. The mule trip took about three hours from Los Teques.

The Rev. Jay Davenport, a tall, lanky missionary, traveled to Paracotos once a month to serve communion, preach and baptize. He was remembered as one who "spoke Spanish using mostly infinitives"! Manuel Key was more often the preacher. A quotation from a diary entry by Rev. Davenport records the intense interest in hearing the Gospel:

"En mis visitas una vez al mes nos congregabamos hasta setenta personas, aunque en programas especiales, como Navidad, reuniamos hasta 140 personas....La mayoria de mis predicaciones en el El Estado Miranda las realizamos en casas humildes, con piso de tierra, sin ventanas, y utilizamos bancos sin espaldas, pero esto en ninguna manera bajaba el espiritu de adoración y devocion.." (Translation: On my visits once a month, we gathered together up to seventy people. For special programs at Christmas, there were up to 140 people. Most of the preaching in the State of Miranda was held in humble huts, with dirt floors and without windows. We used benches without backs, but there was always an atmosphere of reverence.)

A congregation referred to as "La Iglesia del Estado de Miranda" was formed by the newly organized Presbytery of Venezuela in 1946 to include the families of "believers" who were under the care of Rev. Davenport and Sr. Manuel Key. All these families lived on vacant land ("*terrenos baldios*") since the area was made up of several large feudal land estates of the Caracas elites. The first families were nearly all landless peasants.

Our mission residence "Quinta Felicidad"

This was a cement block building with an asbestos sheet roof. There were three bedrooms which opened off a central patio. Curtains served as doors for the bedrooms. The only panes of glass in the house were those in the three outside doors. Windows had screens and iron rods for security which were built into the window frames. Crude wooden blinds could be lowered to keep out the rain. The floors were of cement tinted with green dye.

The house had the only modern bathroom with running water in the village. The water storage tank was mounted on a storage shed which was filled daily with power generated by a gasoline motor. By midday the water was heated by the sun! That provided warm water for a good shower after the afternoon siesta.

Our family usually arose at six in the morning and stayed up until ten or eleven in the evening. The water supply came from our deep water well which was shared with the community through a spigot located about thirty yards from the house along the trail which connected the main road with the remote area known as "La Mata". Women came daily to fill large lard cans and carried them to their homes on their heads.

There were probably only a couple of houses in the village that had cement floors. One of those houses had been the residence of the foreman of the hacienda when it was owned by an absentee landlord. The other houses were built of *bajareque* which was a simple wall construction made from saplings, small stones and plastered with mud mixed with straw and cow dung. Most of the huts had a tin roof, but a few still had a thatched straw roof.

Our favorite tree was the *acacias* with its lovely orange blossoms. Sometimes the large ants stripped the branches bare. The climbing vines on the outside walls of the house were called *bellisima*, literally translated "the most lovely". Hibiscus also grew with their large, gorgeous dark leaves and red blossoms. Zinnias thrived well. Some times we had orchids blooming in the crotch of a low tree or in a hanging basket. The tropical heat and abundant rain made for the rapid growth of the vegetation. The *gamelote*, a thick grass, had to be cut back regularly with a *machete*.

The mules and the donkeys

We inherited three mules and three donkeys from the previous missionary family. These beasts of burden were used for itineration in "the roadless area". The mules were named "Faith, Hope and Charity". "Charity" was a difficult beast which had to be worked every day or she got out of control. "Faith" was a scrawny, ugly little mule, but she turned out to have a good disposition and was very dependable. "Hope" was a big, beautiful animal, but lazy and difficult to handle The donkeys were named after the family of the U.S. President Harry Truman: "Harry", "Bess" and "Margaret."!

PART   FIVE

Services and outreach ministries

EVANGELISM IN THE RURAL VILLAGES

Religious liberty in Venezuela

Since there was freedom of religion in Venezuela, there was no need to request permission to hold a religious service on a street corner and in private properties. However it was wise to visit the local "*jefatura*" (city hall and police station) to advise the authorities that you were a pastor and wanted to conduct an out of doors service or a house meeting in their village. This made sure that there would be a police officer nearby in case there was anyone who might cause disturbances or boys who might toss rocks on the roof.

In most cases, the missionary requested the support of the local authorities since he did not want any public disturbances. Most city officials were supportive of the missionary efforts since they knew that the "*evangelicos*" encouraged obedience to civil authorities and emphasized personal and public morality.

There were usually four traditional ways to evangelize: distribution of tracts and Bibles, house meetings for Bible study, open air evangelism and later radio programs.

The evangelistic service in the open air

The service began with the playing of a hymn on a portable organ or the playing of sacred music on a portable phonograph. Good recorded Gospel music was readily available. Ideal time for an out door service were "the siesta hour" (1 to 3 p.m.) and the early evening (7-9 p.m.). If the sun had set, a gasoline lantern provided enough light to conduct a service.

Hymns were sung by all who could read from the small hymnals. The preacher had to put up with the braying of a donkey, the crowing of a rooster, the passing carts and horses and at times the voices of hecklers. Jesus probably had some of the same problems when He preached in the open air!

The service was made more meaningful by a testimony by a believer who spoke about his or her faith and what faith in Jesus meant to him personally. There was the always a simple sermon with an invitation to anyone who wanted to learn more about the Gospel to stay after the service for conversation.

The house meeting for prayer and Bible study

These were always more effective since the people could sit down and experience a sense of worship and be free from the street noise. Usually in any village there would be at least one home which would open its doors to a visiting evangelist to present the Gospel message and answer questions about the Bible.

The visual charts made teaching more effective. Since many who attended were semi-literate, the use of charts with simple words, symbols and drawings helped greatly in communicating religious concepts.

Free copies of the Gospels and the Psalms were always offered at the close of the service. Some participants simply took the literature and walked away, while others lingered to ask questions or to listen to the answers given to others if they were hesitant to asked questions.

Since most of the ministry of Jesus was done in homes or on the street, this method of evangelism was continuing a method used by Jesus.

Radio programs

During the 1950s a radio station was established in Ocumare. It was a channel for the community for popular culture and a source of local news and information. The owner of the station was a member of the Masonic Order so he was of a liberal persuasion in relation to selling radio time to a Protestant church.. Ramon "Suro" Lara purchased a share in the station when it was organized. Pastor Eugene Lee who came to Venezuela in the mid 1950s had extended experience in radio and mass communications which was a great asset in this missionary outreach..

Pastor Lee organized *"Paginas Campestres"*, a weekly program with an announcer. Usually he brought in "a guest commentator". On one occasion it was Luis Lara, the local sanitation inspector, who spoke on the need to build a modern latrine for each home which the government would provide.

The theme song was "*Adios a Ocumare*" sung by a popular singer, Edith Salgado. The youth of the congregation also had their own program called "*Estampas Juveniles*". The cast was made up of Virgilio Caraballo, Juan Chipamo, Gladys Aleman, Argelia Rivero and Manases Ortega. Occasionally, Juan Chipamo, a seminary student, spoke. "El Sabado de Gloria" (the day before Easter), the presentation was so good that the doctor at the government hospital called to commend him on his message.

Another part of the radio ministry was the recorded Bible verses which were played for a minute as the station came on the air in the morning, again at high noon and in the evening when the station went off the air. Eugene Lee wrote the script for the youth program and often loaned his tape recorder when needed to the radio station. The Bible verses were recorded by excellent native speakers, the Reverends Ramon Gonzalez and Roberto Seel..

DISTRIBUTION OF BIBLES AND CHISTIAN LITERATURE

The historic importance of the printing press

The Western world was impacted profoundly by the invention of the printing press by Gutenberg in the same decade in which Martin Luther posted "The Fifty Theses" on the cathedral door in Wittenberg in 1517. Over one thousand copies of that document were in circulation by 1522! One might have said then 'that the train had left the station in Western Europe! In contrast, in the Arab world, moveable type was not easily adaptable to Arabic letters and also there was little interest in teaching the common people to read. The invention of the printing press served as a catalyst for the spread of knowledge in the West, which was not true in the Eastern world.

The modern literacy movement

The *"Accion Democratica"* government in 1944-48 launched a national literacy campaign with a massive rally in the *"Nuevo Circo"* stadium in Caracas. An adaption of the Laubach literacy method had been developed, using Venezuelan vocabulary and drawings.

In the Tuy Valley the rate of adult illliteracy was probably nearly 60% and the national average was 47%. The time was ripe to go into the public markets with a bookmobile to sell Bibles and basic adult literature as a part of the mission program.

A cabinet for books was built to fit in the back door of the Chevolet "Carry All" van. It was easy to set up. Early in the morning our van would be parked near the entrance of the open air city market. The missionary or church elder was ready to sell Bibles and other literature as the people arrived for market or as they returned home. The price of the literature offered for sale was modest:

- Single copies of the four Gospels and the Psalms sold for three cents:
- Single copies of the Ten Commandments and the Beatitudes – five cents;
- The New Testament sold for one bolivar or thirty-three cents;
- The Bible, artificially leather- bound, cost three bolivars or one dollar.

Tracts were distributed on personal hygiene, farming methods, nutrition, first aid and parental guidance. All these were free.

The schedule for the public markets required that the bookmobile be parked and ready to open for sale by 5 a.m. Over the years thousands of copies of the Scriptures were placed in the hands of the growing literate population. It is hard to under estimate the impact of this program through the sale the of the Holy Scriptures and the distribution of Christian and socially relevant literature in the public market places.

A photo of a young man holding a tract in his hand, surrounded by an old woman and a boy, reflects the interest in receiving literature but also the inability to read what was on the paper. (See this picture in the photo section of the book)

PUBLIC HEALTH IN VENEZUELA IN THE 1950s

The governments of Lopez Contreras and Isaiah Medina began to take seriously the problems of public health in the 1930s and 40s. Malaria was a major problem and DDT was just beginning to become available.

The campaign to eliminate malaria

By the early 1940s a massive spraying campaign was organized which sprayed every dwelling in the nation and marked it with "a DDT number". This number became a permanent house identification number and was also used by the postal and public safety services. It was then not necessary to know a street number if one knew the DDT number of a house or office..

The program to build latrines

A standard sized "out house" was developed. The simple structure was made of concrete slab walls, a door with hinges and an asbestos roof. The pit dug below the latrine was lined to a depth of twenty feet with concrete slabs. There was no "wooden seat" which could transmit infections, but as simple concrete seat that could be scrubbed.

There was no charge for the latrine. At the mission property in Santa Barbara, the public health officer ordered a latrine to be built next to "Jacob's Well" on the mission property. This encouraged those who came to draw water not to relieve themselves "in the bushes"!

The arrival of penicillin and related antibiotics

These new drugs were readily available in the mid 1940s in Venezuela. The ingested pill was being replaced by injected antibiotics so that the medications could be placed directly in the body rather than taken through the mouth. Since illiteracy was high, many people could not read the printed instructions nor did they own a watch to take the medicine on time.

The local public health doctor

Santa Barbara was fortunate to have the services of a series of public health officers who take their work seriously. One doctor had recently served in a rural area in Guatemala with the World Health Organization.   Santa

Barbara was just five miles from the government hospital in Ocumare del Tuy on an all weather road. With the services of the missionary nurse at the Santa Barbara mission clinic, a van to transport patients and the visit of a doctor for free consultation every week, the opportunities for improved health immediately became a blessing for the community.

THE LINK: DEMOCRACY AND EDUCATION

One of the important programs of the *CENTRO CRISTIANO RURAL* was adult education, and in particular, adult literacy. Pastor Sinclair and Maxine who was an experienced public school teacher, were made aware early after their arrival in Venezuela in 1949 that adult literacy was only 47%. The percentage might have been even higher if the standard for being "literate" was only the ability to read traffic signs, bill boards and political slogans. Pastor Sinclair felt that only one in three persons in Santa Barbara was functionally literate.

Adult literacy

How to being was the question? Thanks to the good orientation of the Language and Orientation School they had attended in Colombia before arriving in Venezuela, the Sinclairs had been introduced to the Laubach literacy method. Dr. Laubach had developed the method among the rural people of The Philippines during the early 1940s. The U.S. Information Service in Caracas had begun to distribute basic literature for new Spanish readers through the American Embassy.

The Laubach method was based on four principles: (1) The teacher could be trained to use the method quickly and di not need formal pedagogical education. (2) The method used the visual technique – simple drawings to illustrate words. (3 The vocabulary was related to the routine acts of daily life such as cooking, cleaning, shopping and traveling. For example, words like fire, danger, washing, road signs and basic furniture names were used. (4) A basic story from the Bible was included, such as "The Prodigal Son" which included familiar words: father, son, brother, lost, found, hired man, ring, dead, alive.

Maxine began the adult literacy program with a class of six young adult males. The class was successful, but since she was also committed to home schooling our six-year old son, we had to recruit and train a Venezuelan teacher. The right person came along at the right time. He was Juan Espinoza, a young man of twenty-two who had failed in his first job in Caracas with the YMCA. However he deserved a second chance and was a bright young man and was interested in finding a vocation. Juan immediately responded to the invitation to train to be an adult literacy teacher.

The first six students represented a cross section of the rural community; two were husky, Afro-Venezuelans, who had never had more than a few days of schooling before they were sent out to work in the fields as day laborers They were known as "the Martinez boys". Another was a local landowner who could read a few words but said he only wanted to learn "to write my name".

Education as a foundation of democracy

We need to understand adult education as a vital link to a functioning democracy. One needs to believe that a country with a population of unemployed, illiterate young adults will not be able to embrace democracy. Education works humbly and quietly in societies and rarely gets the credit when change happens. It is not glamorous, Classrooms provide little drama. But little happens in a revolutionary way without education.

After the ouster of General Perez Jimenez in 1958 and the election of President Romulo Betancourt (the first president to finish his term of office), the Banco Agricola offered loans to small family farmers. It was said that after leaving the bank with the loan, the farmer would go to the store and buy first a wrist watch and then a transistor radio. Both would put him immediately in touch with the outside world. It was the beginning of a spiritual, political and economic renewal. (Cf. Lee, Eugene, letter, March 12, 2011)

A flash forward to 2011

In 2011 one can see what is happening in the Arab world when a large group of young, unemployed, but literate youth, rise up and demand change. The World Bank studies report that literacy more than doubled in the region between 1960 and 1995, besting the progress on other world regions. Primary completion rates in Egypt, Tunisia, Jordon and Saudi Arabia all topped 90% in the last decade.

The level of general education has a direct impact on the degree of functional democracy. It seems that that is what happened between 1945 and 1965 in rural Venezuela. The 2000 statistics for literacy in Venezuela is now reported as 93%. (Mission Yearbook, 2011, p. 297)

What actually happens to new adult readers

New readers gain a new sense of well-being which can only be compared to walking out of a dark room into the sun light. The headlines of the newspaper now catch their attention, as do the political slogans on the billboards. They are no longer embarrassed when a political candidate hands them a tract at the village store. This same experience occurs as they open the Bible at church and find (sometimes with help) the page which is being read by the pastor and then know for sure that this is "the Word of God" !

"*Educacion popular*" – Visions of democracy

The Presbyterian Mission was able to secure educational films from the Embassy of the United States of America in Caracas. The Centro Cristiano Rural had a portable 500 watt generator and a movie projector. The missionary could show films on cultural, health and agriculture topics anywhere. He only had to load the equipment on a couple of donkeys,ravel up the trail a few kilometers, set up the equipment and he were ready for the showing. A large white sheet hung on poles served as a screen. The films usually had subtitles in Spanish.

One can only imagine the great interest there was in an isolated village or a "*caserios*" for a film night. There was no need for publicity since the news spread by word of mouth. There would be a crowd camped on a hillside at sundown. The "comics" came first in the program. The operator simply ran the film backwards for a few minutes! What laughter arose from the crowd as the actors in the film climbed up stairs backwards!

After showing the film "Abraham Lincoln: A man of the people"

Ramon and Rafael walked up the trail to their huts after the movie, chatting about all they had learned from this film.

Ramon: You know that President Lincoln grew up in real poverty like us. His family was really "share croppers" like us and our neighbors. And there were also a lot of "politicos" around who were telling the people to just be content with what they had and not to cause trouble!

Rafael: And did you hear that part of his speech at the place where one of the great battles between the states was fought? I think they called that war "La Guerra Civil". It was fought over one hundred years ago.

Ramon: If I remember correctly, that part of the speech went something like this: "We are fighting this war so that we can have "un gobierno del pueblo, para el pueblo y por el pueblo." (A government of the people, for the people and by the people)

Rafael: And then the President added "*para que esta nacion no perezca de la faz de la tierra.* ("So that this nation would not perish from the face of the earth") He said a lot in a few words!

Ramon: I think that we need someone like that Lincoln – or like a leader in China who they call Sun Yat Sen – or even like our Simon Bolivar – a leader who will let the people have a share in making decisions about their future. I am fed up with this "*caciquismo*" *y paternalismo de los gobernantes*".. I am going to write the U.S. Embassy and asked them for a copy of that whole speech in Spanish so I can read it carefully. I think that Jesus would like what we heard tonight since He was always stood up for the poor.

PART SIX

The Roman Catholic Church

and

Evangelical Christianity -

yesterday and today

THE COLONIAL CHURCH

When the Spanish conquistadores arrived in Venezuela, they did not find major population groups and civilizations as in Mexico and Peru, but a bewildering multiplicity of small tribes dispersed over a wide area. The most important group they found in the Colombia and Venezuela region was the "Chibcha" tribe. It is estimated that at the beginning of the sixteenth century they numbered around one million, out of some two and three million indigenous people. Perhaps 300,000 grouped in the coastal region and the mountains. The huge regions of the Plains and the Orinoco and Amazon basins were sparsely populated by small tribes living as gatherers, fishers and hunters.

The Gospel came to Latin America with the sword. The first churchmen to explore the territory did so in their capacity as chaplains to the conquistadores. The Spanish crown required the captains to take at least two priests on all expeditions.

Indians living on the perimeters of the "towns of Spaniards" were gathered to be taught doctrine by the Franciscan and Dominican friars. The church was not as much "the protectors and defenders of Indians" as it set out to be. The missionaries did little to improve the sad lot of native populations which were rapidly decimated by war, forced labor and newly imported diseases, such as smallpox.

(1) Cf. Dussel, Enrique, THE CHURCH IN LATIN AMERICA, 1492 - 1992, pp. 271 – 280. Watters, Mary, A HISTORY OF THE CHURCH IN VENEZUELA, 1810 – 1930; Schwaller, John Frederick, THE HISTORY OF THE CHURCH IN LATIN AMERICA: From conquest to Revolution and beyond"; and Cleary, Edward L., THE RISE OF THE CHARISMATIC CATHOLICISM IN LATIN AMERICA.

Slaves were brought from West Africa to work in the gold mines, pearl fisheries and the great estates of sugar cane, cacao and cattle. There were some honorable exceptions of the Spanish clergy, such as Alonso de Sandoval (1576 – 1632) and his disciple, Pedro Claver who died in Cartegena in 1654 who sided with the patriots.

The Catholic Church controlled behavior, dictated discourse on the meaning of life and accompanied the faithful from cradle to grave. It paced daily life to the sound of church bells and gave shape to the year with numerous feast days. The bable of Amerindian languages was enough to discourage even the most competent linguist. To take an example, on the Plains of Caracas there were about thirty native peoples, each with its own language and none were written.

The Church also had control of education and public charity. A seminary was founded in Caracas in 1673 which was raised to university status in 1717. There was a complete union between throne and altar, but never entirely free of conflict. This troublesome inheritance caused the Church to pay dearly in the republican period when it lost much of its control.

THE CHURCH IN THE INDEPENDENCE STRUGGLE AND UNDER THE REPUBLIC

The wars of independence (1810 – 21) shook the Catholic Church violently and caused it to divide openly. Most of the bishops remained loyal to the Spanish king. However among the native clergy was a strong group on the side of "the patriots". They were increasingly resentful of the virtual monopoly of high ecclesiastical offices held by the "penisular" clergy. When the moment came in 1810 for the "Colombian Act of Independence", sixteen out of fifty-three signatories were clergy who signed the Venezuelan Act.

The Church was deeply affected by the struggle. Church property was subject to frequent sackings by one side or the other. Clergy numbers dropped markedly as seminaries closed, priests were killed in fighting, ordinations dried up and religious were expelled from their convents. The figures from the Diocese of Caracas give an idea of the scale of this: there were 547 clergy in 1810 and only 110 in 1819.

The Church was weakened, but clerical participation on the side of the emancipation cause earned it a prominent place in the new society. However conflicts soon appeared as the new state placed limits to the social influence of the Church. A time of tensions between Church and state was beginning.

The Catholic Church's confrontation with the liberals was more conflictive in Venezuela than in Colombia and Ecuador. This confrontation reached a climax during the rule of the liberal Antonio Guzman Blanco (1870 – 88) by the end of which the Church was exhausted. Under the dictatorship of Juan Vicente Gomez (1908 – 35) party leaders and public freedoms were abolished and the persecution of the Church came to an end. Gomez applied the Patronage law rigorously and kept strict control of the clergy.

AN ASSESSMENT OF THE INFLUENCE OF THE CHURCH IN VENEZUELA

In an incisive analysis of the influence of the Church in Venezuela, historian Mary Watters, pointed out that certain restrictions commonly placed on the church by anti-clerical legislators have never been enacted in Venezuela. The institution has never been entirely dispossessed of its property by state expropriation. The clergy may establish schools, although schools must submit to public inspection and regulations. The political privileges of the clergy have been maintained. This may be attributed to the equalitarian sentiment of the people which has persisted since 1810.

The majority of the Venezuelan intelligentsia regarded the reduction of the influence of the church as a cause for national congratulation. Vallenilla Lanz asserted "In the psychological state of our people, religion and morals are so closely united that to destroy the one is to attack fatally the other".(Watters, p.. 224)

The Law of the Patronage has remained the most stable political instrument Venezuela in its legal heritage.

THE PRESENCE OF NORTH AMERICAN ROMAN CATHOLIC MISSIONAIES IN LATIN AMERICA IN THE 1940s AND 1950s.

"A Call for Forty Thousand" was published by J.J. Considine, M.M., in 1946, under the imprimatur of Archbishop Spellman. His insights into the need of Latin American Catholicism for a new missionary crusade resulted in significant contingents of apostolic workers from the United States of North America assigned to serve in Latin America. There was a revival of the lay apostolate in Latin America through mission agencies such as The Company of St. Paul, The Grail, the Association for International Development (known as A.I.D.), Papal Volunteers for Latin America (PAVLA) and other movements. A goal was set in 1965 to send one thousand American priests and religious workers to Latin America. These movements had a marked effect on the renewed vitality of the Roman Catholic Church in Venezuela.. (Note: One of these new recruits, Ray Pinard, fell in love with a delightful young missionary teacher from Texas who was serving with the Presbyterian mission.)

THE CATHOLIC CHURCH AFTER THE SECOND VATICAN COUNCIL (1959 – 1963)

Venezuela had changed from an agrarian society to an urban industrial society which was based on oil and iron. The Church came into this new age poor in resources due to the elimination of tithes and the confiscation of much of its property. It was forced to reduce its social commitments. It was also faced with a residual anti-clericalism. When the Christian-Social party (COPEI) came to power in 1968, the changes of outlook which had been produced by the Second Vatican Council and the Medellin Conference found the Church in better health than at any stage in the 150-year history of the Republic.

Two continuing challenges for the Catholic Church

Two recent books on the Church in Latin America are worthy of note: a history of the church by Dr. Schwaller and a publication on the Catholic Charismatic movement by Father Edward J.Cleary. (See bibliography pages)

Dr.Schwaller traces the major themes and issues of the Catholic Church from Columbus to the present. This is a difficult task for a region which today comprises eighteen countries, each with its own understanding of its distinctive history. He affirms that the Catholic Church has been "the central institution" in the history of Latin America from the priest's rebellion against Cortes in Mexico and more recently with the Chilean dictator Augusto Pinochet's confrontation with Cardinal Raul Silva Henriquez.

The other major challenge is treated by Father Cleary in THE RISE OF CHARISMATIC CATHOLICISM IN LATIN AMERICA. He points our that "the 35 million Latin Americans which have turned to the Catholic Charismatic Movements (CCR) are more than twice the number which have joined the ranks of the Catholic Charismatic movements."

The questions today are: "Has Pentecostalism transformed Latin American Protestantism as a grass roots movement committed to evangelization? Does this also have the potential to revitalize the Catholic Church?

These are two vital factors in the future for both Evangelical Christianity (Protestantism) and Roman Catholicism in Venezuela in the coming decades.

AN HISTORICAL FOOTNOTE

An example of the dramatic change in attitudes toward Protestants is reflected in the translation of this pastoral letter from the parish priest in Ocumare del Tuy because of the presence of the small Presbyterian congregation in the Mendoza Agricultural Colony in 1951.

"To the faithful in the Mendoza Colony:
My purpose in writing you is to warn you of the outrageous Evangelical heresy which has invaded our region. When the Evangelicals pass with their cowardly smiles, close your doors and make the sign of the cross on your brow and breast, because a message of sin, blasphemy and hell is approaching you.

What is Protestantism? It is a bunch of lies invented by Luther and others in the 16th century. However it is the Catholic Church which has existed for over sixteen hundred years and enlightened the world with the holiness of life. Luther blasphemed the Most Holy Mother of God, the Virgin Mary and the Blessed Patriach St. Joseph. He denied even that there was a hell and thereby fell into the abyss of damnation.

Dear faithful of the Colony, the Virgin Carmen will be in your village, going from house to house to defend you from these blasphemies and sin. They come in sheep's clothing but are in fact ravenous wolves. As they pass by your door, looking for whom they might devour, close the door, make the sign of the cross and flee from these hungry wolves. God bless you.
Father Jose Boleiro, O.P. Ocumare del Tuy.

PROTESTANTISM IN VENEZUELA

Early beginnings

Evangelical Christianity (Protestantism) was established in Venezuela in the early 19th century. The beginnings grew out of the presence of citizens from predominantly Protestant countries who came as soldiers, merchants, diplomats and educators. They pressed the revolutionary governments for liberty of religion as a basic democratic guarantee.

Among these were the English doctors and soldiers who came with the British Legion during the wars of independence, 1810-1825. The family of a British doctor, Robert Irwin, was one of the first to settle in Venezuela. His descendents are to be found today in the church leadership and in several key positions in public life.

There were English teachers recruited by Joseph Lancaster to establish primary schools, using the Bible as a basic text for instruction. Lancaster was invited by General Simon Bolivar in 1825 and remained for several years in Caracas.

Colporteurs were sent by the British and Foreign Bible Society and the American Bible Society in the same period. They sold Bibles in the public markets as well as from door to door. One of the most noted was Canut de Bon, a colorful ex-Catholic friar, who was untiring in his efforts in the 1850s to sell the Holy Scriptures "to the high and the low bred" of society.

A Scottish trading settlement was established in 1825 in the Topo River Valley to the northwest of the Port of La Guaira. Even though that colony of Scots lasted for only a few years, their presence and the ministry of their chaplains left its imprint. Some Scots married into Venezuelan families.

The first permanent congregations

A Methodist missionary arrived in 1887 and organized "La Iglesia del Mesias" in Caracas whose members included Professor Heraclio Osuna who arrived in 1890 from exile in Bogota where he had embraced the Protestant faith. He founded the Colegio Americano of Caracas in 1895.

He was joined that same year by the Rev. and Mrs. Pond, Presbyterian missionaries who were transferred from Barranquilla, Colombia to work in Caracas. About the same time, the Rev. Bailey of the Plymouth Brethren (English) established a congregation in downtown Caracas, near the National Capitol.

La Iglesia Presbiteriana "El Redentor" was organized in 1897 with fourteen members and continues to today as the "Principe de Paz" congregation. This congregation is the oldest continuing Evangelical congregation in Venezuela.

The Orinoco River Mission, The New Tribes Mission, The Southern Baptist Mission, the Evangelical Free Mission and the Scandinavian Missionary Alliance came in later years to work across the length and breadth of the nation.

Congregations in the State of Miranda

Presbyterian missionaries and lay evangelists began to itinerate in the State of Miranda which surrounded the Federal District in 1924. The Rev. Harold Davenport traveled by mule to Paracotos and as far as Ocumare del Tuy. He organized worshipping groups which met in homes. For a short time, the lay evangelist Manuel Key lived in Paracotos.

It was not until the mid 1930s when the Mendoza Rural Development Project was initiated in the Upper Tuy Valley that a small group of Evangelical families gathered for worship in the section of this agricultural colony known as "Santa Barbara". Among the first families were the Juan Espinoza and Salome Martinez families.

In 1946 "La Iglesia del Buen Pastor" was formally organized in Santa Barbara and become a member of the newly organized Presbytery of Venezuela, later to become La Iglesia Evangelica Presbiteriana de Venezuela. Pastor C. Paul Russell took up residence in Santa Barbara with his family in 1947 and was assigned a fourteen acre plot as "un colono" with water rights to the new government irrigation system. This gifted missionary had a farm background from the United States and was also a medical technician who could prescribe medicine and give injections.

A continuing missionary presence for six decades

Across the years from 1947 to 2005, six missionary couples and one missionary nurse served in this field:

> Rev. and Mrs.(Bodine) C. Paul Russell (1947 – 1951)
> Rev. and Mrs. (Maxine) John H. Sinclair (1951 – 1956)
> Ms. Mary J. Armbruster, R.N. (1051 – 1960)
> Rev. and Mrs. Eugene (Jeanne Marie) Lee (1952 – 60)
> Rev. and Mrs. (Jean and Betty Mae) Robert E. Seel (1960s)
> Rev. and Mrs. (Joyce) Paul Bock (1970 – 75)
> Reverends Carlos and Deborah Clugy-Soto (1991 – 2005)

In addition to these missionaries there were always a cadre of willing lay leaders to carry on the work. The mission could never have been successful without the untiring service of volunteer lay workers.

Four mission institutions

A leading researcher on Protestantism in Latin America, Professor Jean Pierre Bastian, considers that the most missionary strategies have included: a local congregation, a school, a printing press and medical work. (Cf. Bastian, pp. 102 – 110). The results of these strategies have been successfuil beyond the imagination.

In 2010 the Protestant community was estimated at 3,052,000 or about six percent of a population of 29, 243,555 according to OPERATION WORLD, published by the International Institute of Christian Studies. The Roman Catholic community is estimated at seventy-one percent. In most countries in Latin America, there is no attempt to identify religious preferences in official a national census.

PART SEVEN

VENEZUELA - 2012

VENEZUELA – 2012

2011 was the 200th anniversary of the Independence of the nation

Hugo Chavez Frias, the 61st President of Venezuela, holds full sway today in the Palacio Nacional de Miraflores in Caracas. The old tiled-roof town that had existed for three hundred and fifty years is gone. General Marcos Perez Jimenez (1948 -1958) plundered the resources of the nation without even sharing it equitably with the rest of the military! He squandered much of it on fancy building projects. Above all he left a trail of graft and corruption, even though he received in 1955 the Legion of Merit medal from the government of the United States.

Today, a half century later and after a series of left and right- center political parties which have ruled for more than thirty years, a brash, modern city with dazzling white skyscrapers sparkles against a green Andean backdrop. Corruption also has grown apace with the skyscrapers.

The gap between the rich and poor continues to widen and has triggered growing popular protests. Even though the statistics show a rise in per capita income, in 1983 the Archbishop of Caracas decried the low wages, the denial of worker rights and the absence of social services for the poor. He declared that "the immense masses live in conditions which cannot be regarded as human" (Cf. Tariq, Ali, "Pirates in the Caribbean", p. 47-48.

The rise of a new "caudillo"

Hugo Chavez was born on July 28, 1954 to "dirt poor" elementary school teacher parents in Sabaneta, Barinas. He grew up to become another kind of "caudillo". His brand of "revolución bolivariano" has emerged as a mixture of "socialismo, messianismo and caudillismo" Over nearly two decades in power, he has spawned an era of cronyism and corruption. Certainly there has been a reduction in poverty, and a significant redistribution of wealth, but the future of Venezuela is still an enigma.. He has been called "Hugo Hurricane" – a one-man whirlwind.

Chavez's parents were the latest in a line of guerilla fighters. His great-great grandfather, Colonel Pedro Perez Perez was a guerilla who fought against the principal landowners who ruled Venezuela in the 1840s. As the son of school teachers, Chavez was given a love of reading and learning. He graduated first in his high school class. However his first love was baseball. He longed to be a major league pitcher. After an arm injury abruptly ended Hugo's dream of a baseball stadium, he graduated from the Military Academy in 1975 and joined an elite unit of the paratroopers, ascending to the rank of colonel lieutenant. Later he left active duty and returned to the military academy as chief sports instructor.

As to religion, Hugo Chavez was raised Catholic, but is not a regular church attender. He often mentions Jesus Christ – perhaps as often as he quotes Simon Bolivar! He received a blessing from Pope Benedict XVI in 2006 and sees himself as "a modern Messiah". A recent biographer wrote: "He is religious in the way that serves his political project".(Cf. Jeff C. Young, Hugo Chavez:: leader of Venezuela", 2006.)

The "Revolución Bolivariano – 200" movement

The "200" was added since 1983 was the 200th anniversary of the birth of Simon Bolivar. Hugo Chavez has created "de facto" a huge welfare state. In a nation of 26 million people, 2 million Venezuelans are government employees. Chavez's program includes free university education, subsidized food and cash benefits for single mothers.

Chavez also appointed a commission to create a national curriculum that taught students that "collectivism" is preferable to "individualism". He has also grabbed control of Venezuela's vast natural resources of oil and minerals.

In the agricultural field, he designated four million acres for land redistribution in farm cooperatives. He embraces and praises socialism, but also acts much like a capitalist when it came to making oil deals. His character is unpredictable to say the least.

Chavez in the international arena

In 2005 at the summit in Argentina of presidents of thirty-three Latin American nations along with George W. Bush, he opposed the Free Trade Area of the Americas in a two hour speech. In that discourse he offered a $10 billion decade-long assistance program to eliminate hunger in Latin America.

Chavez was wise enough to know that there is "a culture of corruption" which is deeply imbedded in Latin America. He called this culture "a monster with a thousand heads and to slay it will not be easy". In Venezuela, *"palanca"* (a personal connection) is often more important in landing a job than education or qualifications.

He has developed relations with China, making four trips there. He has become involved in the purchase of eighteen tankers to facilitate getting the oil to China which is forty-five days by sea.

In relation to the State of Miranda, he has sparked the growth of two "bedroom communities" – Cua and Los Teques . He built the first railroad in seventy years from Caracas to Cua and spent $850 million to build a subway from Caracas to Los Teques.

Chavez is now in the forefront of a new wave of leftists across Latin America and the world. He trots the globe, visiting Fidel Castro, Saddam Hussein and Evo Morales. He echoes the struggle of the underclass everywhere – from Caracas to Harlem, to Johannesburg and to Bombay. He declares "a new path" which is between "a savage capitalism" and "a failed communism". He is a leader in a new regionalism in the developing world. The Latin American region is entering a new phase of its history, one marked by higher levels of development, intraregional rivalries and an increasing degree of geopolitical autonomy. (Cf. "Rethinking Latin America" in FOREIGN AFFAIRS, March-April, 2012.)

In a 2008 interview with journalists Douglas Brinkley, Christopher Hutchins and actor Sean Penn, Chavez was asked several key questions.

Q. Should the Monroe Doctrine be abolished? A. The Monroe Doctrine has to be broken. We've been stuck with it for 200 years.

Q. What's the difference between you and Fidel Castro? A. Fidel is a communist. I am not. Fidel is a Marxist-Leninist. I am not. Fidel is an atheist. I am a Christian. I believe in the Social Gospels of Christ. He doesn't.

Q. If Barack Obama is elected President of the United States, would you be willing to fly to Washington and meet him? A. Yes.. Fidel wants me to call him after we have spoken…He wants to know everything we speak about.

Later in the conversation, Chavez brings up another possibility for a meeting place. He suggested they meet in Guantanamo Bay: "Perhaps we could talk and then send him home with a gift – say, the American flag that waves over Guantanamo Bay!" (Cf. "NATION, December 2, 2008.)

Chavez has been outspoken in his criticism of the opposition. He has called former President George W. Bush "an illegitimate president" because of the controversial election of 2000. He also called him "the devil" in an address at the United Nations, and accused him of "talking as if he owned the world". Yet Venezuela needs the income that comes from selling oil to the U.S. as much as the U.S. needs the oil. Only Canada, México and Saudi Arabia export more oil to the U.S. According to a 2004 estimate, Venezuela has oil reserves of 77.8 billion barrels; the U.S. has only 22 billion of oil reserves.

In the first months of 2012, Chavez is still widely popular and leads his opponent, Henrique Capriles, in recent surveys. However undecided voters are still more critical to Chavez to win the October 7 election.

In summary, Chavez is a symbol of an historic shift of power to the long-exploited brown-skinned poor. The Venezuelans now seem to be in control of their own country for the first time since the Spanish conquest four centuries ago, according to Chavez. Only time will confirm this historic shift.

CHAPTER SEVEN

"Venezuela – 2012"

Hugo Chavez – the day after the coup d'etat and the
General listening to the concerns of citizens

Fidel Castro turned into Chávez's main mentor, provoking worries among Venezuela's upper classes that Chávez planned to turn the oil giant into a twenty-first-century version of the Communist-run island. But while Chávez and Castro were allies, sharp differences separated their social experiments. (AP/Wide World Photos)

A day after the coup, photographers caught a glimpse of military officials transferring Chávez at the Fort Tiuna military base. Ever the voracious reader, he carried that day's newspapers and other material. (AP/Wide World Photos)

When floods hit the frontier town of Guasdualito in Apure state in 2002, Chávez visited to listen to residents' concerns and help direct relief efforts. (Agencia Bolivariana de Noticias)

AN AFTERWORD

Now in the year 2012 and looking back over sixty years to the 1950's, we ask "What has changed in the Upper Tuy Valley since then?"; and "What has not changed?" "Is faith still at work to promote freedom and an authentic democratic society?"

The close of a foreign missionary presence

The ministry of Presbyterian missionaries formerly ended with the departure of the Reverends Carlos and Deborah Clugy-Soto in 2005. They concluded fourteen year of service in Venezuela, after spending six years in Africa in the Democratic Republic of the Congo.

The landscape has changed and the population in the area has grown from an estimated 50,000 to 300,000 in the 2010 census. The census showed that the total population of Venezuela is now over 26 million. About 10,000 of these new residents in the Upper Tuy Valley are flood survivors from the coast who were relocated in and around Ocumare. The photos show the skyline of Ocumare with a fourteen story building. The city of Santa Barbara now has paved, lighted streets.

There are a dozen or more Evangelical churches in the area now, while in 1946, there was only one congregation. A Presbyterian pastor reported last year the baptism of twenty babies (and only seven funerals !), seventy new members confirmed and new social programs, such as soup kitchen, clothing closet and a medical clinic in the Los Altos de Altamira.

The dream of a functioning democracy still remains to be achieved after the ten year government of Hugo Chavez. He is now dealing with terminal cancer and a possible successor is not in sight. What does the future hold for Venezuela, especially for the once remote, rural State of Miranda?

WILL FAITH AND FREEDOM TRIUMPH ?

Today's world is on the march to an improved life everywhere. The words of Tom Brokaw in his recent book expresses this challenge in these words:

'The hard work of constantly improving life in this precious planet requires people willing to put boots on the ground, get their hands dirty and spend nights in scary places." (Brokaw, Tom, THE TIME OF OUR LIVES, Random House, New York, 2010. p. 291),

CHAPTER EIGHT

THE STORIES 'RETOLD' IN PHOTOS

AND

PAINTINGS

CHAPTER ONE   "The Little Venice"

Santa Rosa de Aguas, a small village near Maracaibo where the first explorers landed in the 15th century.

One of the first railroads built to connect the Port of La Guaira with Caracas
in the early 20th century

"El Redentor" Presbyterian Church, Condo a Piñango, Caracas, c. 1951

The national "Capitólio" in Caracas. c. 1951

"La Cañada de la Iglesia" barrio, Caracas, c. 1951

The vegetable and fruit vendor

The Venezuela Youth Fellowship Team, 1952
Amanda Pacheco de Jimez, Oda Hilda Gonzalez, Antonio Rivero
and John H. Sinclair

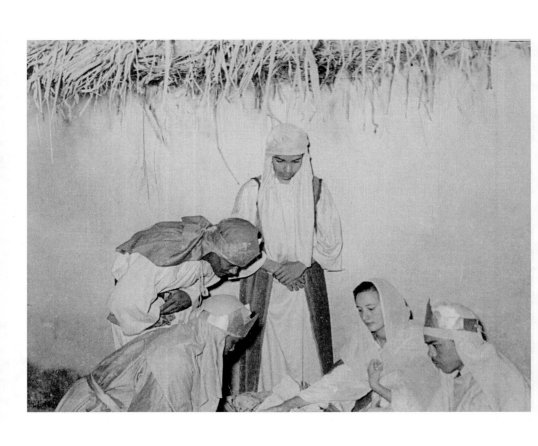

A crèche presentation at the Youth Center, Caracas
1950

Boys singing *"aguinaldos"* on a city street at Christmas time

CHAPTER THREE

VIGNETTES OF THEIR NEIGHBORS

The "Greek merchants" and wives gathered with the Sinclair family at
the Santa Barbara missionary residence
c. 1951

Juan Espinoza constructing a rustic desk at the Siquiri school
c. 1951

CHAPTER FOUR

"The Santa Barbara congregation
and
the Centro Cristiano Rural"

Elder Hipolito Espinoza at the door of the church
1951

The new "El Buen Pastor" church in construction. 1955

John greeting worshippers after the morning service
Santa Barbara, 1953

"El sancocho" served on banana leaves at the Annual Assembly
C.1951

Rev. and Mrs. John P. Sinclair (John's parents) visit the Rivero family at the Rivero home in 1950. Maxine and David joined the Josefina de Rivero and their five children in this photo. Antonio Rivero was the photographer.

Plastering the wall of a house with a bamboo framework
c. 1951

The view of the farm and buildings of the
Christian Rural Center, Santa Barbara

Ramon Lara preaching at *"El Buen Pastor"* Church
Santa Barbara, 1953

Maxine teaching a Sunday School Class
C.1951

Children walking up the hill to church
1951

Youth enjoying games at the missionary residence
1951

The community well, known as "El Pozo de Jacob"
1951

"The Bible Club" with the Christian flag
C.1951

The laying of the cornerstone of the new church building
1955

An ox cart on the trail passing "Quinta Felicidad" (background)
C.1951

Three farm laborers beside a banana tree
C.1951

The clinic and nurse's residence
1951

John at "el pilon" with some Santa Barbara women observing
c. 1951

Plowing with a primitive plow and yoke of oxen

"Mama Blanca" Espinoza carrying home "el agua del dia"
c. 1951

Santa Barbara women and girls learning to quilt with Maxine

Extracting juice from sugar cane.

A pack train along a graveled highway.

Young men receiving a Gospel tract.

John making a home visit in a rural village

CHAPTER FIVE

"Service and outreach ministries"

John visiting an isolated family of a father and two bachelor sons
with Ramon Lara. Senor.   1951

Pastor Efrain Alvarado and Elder Hipolito Espinoza pause in the shade of a bamboo grove.   1951

John on the trail to El Chorreron on "Esperanza" with "Faith coming behind loaded with the baggage.   1951

A preaching service on a village street
1951

An evening service with gasoline lantern in Higuerote, State of
Miranda with seminary student.   1951

A Bible study at noon in an improvised "chapel" on a street corner
Cupira, State of Miranda, 1951

The "Chevy Carry All" driving up the Siquiri River in the dry season
1951

The temporary chapel constructed in Siquiri used for literacy
classes and worship services
c. 1951

John selling Bibles and other books in the Ocumare public market
1951

Church youth with John distributing Christian literature on street
1951

PART TWO

THE RAMON AND MARIA STORY

AND

THE ANTONIO AND MARY STORY

087 Ramon and Maria at the door of their home   1997

John visits Ramon and Maria in their home. 1997

The "recognition service" of Ramon Lara as "pastor emeritus". 2011

THE FAMILY OF RAMON AND MARIA LARA
NEHEMIAS (1)

DANIELA (2) JOSE GREGORIO (3) CARMEN (4) A GGrandaughter (5)

VALENTINA (9)

OMAR (6)

ANILIA (10)

GISEL (7)

GIBLEY (8)

1. Nehemias - son
2. Daniela - grandaughter
3. Jose Gregorio – grandson
4. Carmen - grandaughter

5. A great grandaugther
6. Omar - son
7. Gisel - grandaughter
8. Gibley - grandaughter
9. Valentina- grandaughter
10. Anilia – grandaughter

Antonio Rivero and Mary de Rivero
c. 1988

John and Maxine visit Antonio and Mary
in their home in Tampa, Florida   c. 2003

"Street scene in Quiripital, Estado Miranda"
Watercolor paintings by Antonio Rivero

"In times of trial, He is invisible, but always there"
Watercolor by Antonio Rivero

"An *araguaney* tree in full bloom"
Watercolor by Antonio Rivero

A young Venezuelan mother and child
Watercolor by Antonio Rivero
1953

"The girl drummer"
Watercolor paintings by Antonio Rivero

"The Cross shines even in stormy weather"
Oil painting by John H. Sinclair

"A piñata party"

Maxine, David and Paul with "Bobby Socks". Santa Barbara, 1953

The author with a group of the congregation. The banner reads:

"Welcome to the Iglesia Evangelica Presbiteriana "El Buen Pastor"

"Persevering and Ministering in the Faith"

Young people and children in new sanctuary.

The sign at the entrance to the Centro Cristiano Rural
with Senora Dorotea de Orasma and son

Entrance to the Jubilee Center, Santa Barbara, Ocumare del Tuy

The dormitories and class room at the Jubilee Center
Santa Barbara, Ocumare del Tuy

Carlos and Deborah Clugy-Soto with Jefferson and Jodimar.
2004

APPENDICES, DISCUSSION GUIDE

AND

BIBLIOGRAPHY

BIBLIOGRAPHY

Bastian, Jean Pierre, BREVE HISTORIA DEL PROTESTANTISMO EN LA AMERICA LATINA, CUPSA, Mexico City, 1986, pp.190

Brokaw, Tom, THE TIME OF OUR LIVEDS, Random House, New York, 2010, pp. 291.
Cleary, Edward J., THE RISE OF CHARISMATIC CATHOLICISM IN LATIN AMERICA, Gainesville, University Press of Florida, 2011, xiii,309
Dussel, Enrique, General editor, THE CHURCH IN LATIN AMERICA; 1492 – 1992. Maryknoll, NY, Orbis Books, 1992., pp. 501.
Jones, Bart, HUGO! THE HUGO CHAVEZ STORY: From mud hut to perpetual revolution, Steerforth Press, Hanover, NH, 2007, pp 570
Liscano, Juan, FOLKLORE Y CULTURA, Caracas, Libreria Pensamiento Vivo, 1950, pp. 263.

OPERATION WORLD, Jason Mandryk, editor. Overland Park, KS, IICS, 2010, pp. 978
Phillips, C. Arthur, A HISTORY OF THE PRESBYTERIAN CHURCH IN VENEZUELA, 1958. Unpublished mss., pp. 72

Sales Perez, COSTUMBRES VENEZOLANOS. "Viajes a los Valles del Tuy", Caracas, Librería Pensamiento Vivo, 1946

Seel, Robert E., VENEZUELAN SOJOURN, 1995. Privately printed. pp. 123.Translated by Robert E. Seel, JORNADA PRESBITERIANA, Edited by Edgar Moros Ruano, 2012.
Sinclair, John H., HISTORIA GENERAL DE LA IGLESIA EN LA AMERICA LATINA, Salamanca, Ediciones Sigueme, 1981, Vol. VII, Colombia and Venezuela,
Schwaller, John Frederick, THE HISTORY OF THE CATHOLIC CHURCH IN LATIN AMERICA: From conquest to Revolution and Beyond., New York, New York University Press, 2011, ix, 318.

HISTORIA GENERAL DE LA IGLESIA EN AMERICA LATINA, Vol. VII, "Colombia y Venezuela", Salamanca, Ediciones Sigueme, 1981
VENEZUELA: 1897 - 1927. The Venezuela Mission, 1927. Privately printed., Caracas, pp.31

VENEZUELA: 1897 - 1927. The Venezuela Mission, 1927. Privately printed., Caracas, pp.31

A VENEZUELAN READER. Olivia Burlinghame Goumbri, editor, Washington, D.C., EPICA, 2005, pp.176

VENEZUELA HEROICA, XI Edición, cf. The introduction written by José Martí on the first page.

ANTOLOGIA DEL CUENTO MODERNO VENEZOLANO, 1895 – 1935. Tomo I and Tomo II, 1940, Caracas, Biblioteca Venezolana de Cultura, pp. 348 and pp.204.

Watters, Mary, A HISTORY OF THE CHURCH IN VENEZUELA , 1810- 1930, Chapel Hill, The University of North Carolina Press, 1933, pp. 260

Sinclair, John Henderson, THE STORY OF MY LIFE. Privately published. 1990. Vol. I, pp 202: Vol. II. Pp. 212

Sinclair, John Henderson. PROTESTANTISM IN LATIN AMERICA: A Bibliographical Guide, Pasadena, CA, William Carey Press, 1976. pp. 416

Sinclair, John Henderson, CONVERSATIONS WITH ROMAN CATHOLICS AND THE LATIN AMERICAN CHURCHES, Address at the study conference of the Committee on Cooperation in Latin America, November 5-6, 1961, pp.18.

PRESBYTERIAN MISSION YEARBOOK, Presbyterian Church, USA, 2012 – 13, Louisville, KY, Witherspoon Press, 2012, pp.290

MISSIONARIES/ FRATERNAL WORKERS AND OTHERS WHO CAME FROM ABROAD TO WORK WITH THE PRESBYTERIAN CHURCH OF VENEZUELA/ PRESBYTERIAN MISSION IN VENEZUELA   (1895 – 2012)

Rev. and Mrs. Theodore S. Pond
Rev. and Mrs. Frederick F. Darley
Ms. Lena May Wilson
Rev. and Mrs. Jay F. Davenport
Rev. and Mrs. Merlyn A. Chappel

Rev, and Mrs. (Maud) C. Arthur Phillips
Ms. Verna A. Phillips
Ms. Dorothy M. Parnell
Ms. Margaret Rudy
Ms. Florence E. Yerkins
Ms. Margo Lee Lewis
Ms. Lillian Hanson

Rev.and Mrs. T. Bancroft Reifsnyder
Rev. and Mrs. Calvin H Schmidt
Rev. and Mrs. (Gabriele) John R. Gosney
Rev. and Mrs.(Jean) Scotland
Rev. and Mrs. (Bodine) C. Paul Russell
Rev. and Mrs. (Maxine) John H. Sinclair
Rev. and Mrs. (Jean / Betty Mae) Robert E. Seel;
Rev. and Mrs. (Rosena) Harry Peters
Rev. and Mrs. Allen Clark
Rev. and Mrs. (Irene) James Cavin
Rev. and Mrs. (Jean Marie) Eugene W. Lee
Mr. and Mrs. (Nancy) Stenburg

Rev. and Mrs. (Lolly) Billy Bob Shiflett
Rev. and Mrs. (Joyce) Paul Bock
Rev. and Mrs. (Mary Ellen) McKowen
Rev. and Mrs. Alvin (Anna) Hui
Rev. and Mrs. Joás Dias de Araujo
Rev. and Mrs. (Pauline) Schutmaat
Rev. and Mrs. (Donna) Moros Ruano

Rev. and Mrs. (Deborah) Carlos Clugy-Soto
Dr. and Mrs.(Clare) Alan H. Hamilton
Rev. and Mrs. (Jennie) Williamson

Ms. Jane E. Evans, R.N.
Ms. Constance E. Nissen, R.N.
Ms. Mary J. Armbruster, R.N. (later married Antonio Rivero)
Ms. Evelina Caldwell, R.N.
Mr. and Mrs. Scott (Gloria Romero) Downing

Ms. Vivian Collier (married Ray Pinard)
Mr. Howard Dekalb
Mr. Richard L. Turner, Jr.
Rev. Francisco Ordoñez (Colombia)
Rev. Israel Morales Mata (Guatemala)
Rev. Ramón Gonzalez (Puerto Rico)
Rev. Pablo Guerra (Venezuela/Cuba)
Rev. Humberto Reyes L. (Chile)
Rev. Gustavo Astudillo (Colombia)
Rev. Alfonso Lloreda (Colombia)
Rev. Nicanor Gonzalez (Puerto Rico)
Sr. Arturo Torres (Colombia)
Rev. Simon Benjamin (Costa Rica)

MISSIONARIES who served in the Upper Tuy River Valley

Rev. and Mrs. C. Paul (Bodine) Russell, 1946-51

Rev. and Mrs. John H. (Maxine) Sinclair, 1951-56

Rev. and Mrs. Eugene (Jeanne Marie) Lee, 1952-60

Rev. and Mrs. Robert E. (Jean) Seel   (1957 - 58)

Rev.\and Mrs. Paul (Joyce) Bock (1958-63)

Rev. and Mrs. Carlos (Deborah) Clugy-Soto, 1991 – 2005

MISSION BOARD SECRETARIES (New York mission board office)

Dr. L.K. Anderson, 1942 – 1950

Dr. W. Stanley Rycroft, 1950 – 1960

Rev. John H. Sinclair, 1960 – 73

Rev. Benjamin Gutierrez, 1973 – 1996

Rev. Eriberto Soto, 1996 – 2000

Rev. Tricia Lloyd-Sidle (2000 – 2010)

Ms. Maria Arroyo (2008 -

(Note: After 2010, the Latin America mission supervisary responsibilities
   were divided into several secretarial staff)

FIELD REPRESENTATIVE (field supervisors)

Dr. Harold B. Meyer
Dr. Donald Fletcher

Newly commissioned missionaries of "The Gospel of our Lord Jesus Christ" departing from the Newark, NJ airport for Colombia and Venezuela.

John, Maxine and David Sinclair

160

Members of the Venezuela Mission: C.A. Philips, Maude Philips, Paul Russell, Bodine Russell, Mary Armbruster, Dorothy Parnell, Verna Philips, James Scotland, Jean Scotland, John Sinclair, Maxine Sinclair. Present also was Norman Taylor, mission board area supervisor. John Sinclair was the photographer. 1951

Women missionaries of the Presbyterian Mission at the Colegio
Americano, Caracas: Left to right: Clare Hamilton, Verna Phillips,
Maxine Sinclair, Bodine Russell, Maude Phillips, Jean Scotland
And Jean Seel. (Absent: Mary Armbruster). C. 1951

Presbytery gathering at the Colegio Americano. Near table:
Antonio Merino, Robert Seel, Abelardo Cuadra, Pedro Ponce,
Saturnino Lopez, Antonio Piccardo and Efrain Alvarado;
Middle table: Ray Lopez, Ismael Lugo, Juan Aular, Rufo
Mendoza, Estanislao Rondon, Manuel Key;
Far table: Alfonso Lloreda, Sara Sifuentes, Felix Ruh, C.A.
Phillips, Harry Peters, unidentified elder, c. 1951

Pastors and elders of the Presbytery at the door of the bookstore.
Camino Bolero a Bolero # 6-3, Caracas. c. 1951.

Back row: woman elder, Rev. Alfonso Lloreda, Rev. Juan Aular,
women elder, Sr. Rafael Perez;
Middle row: Rev. Rufo Mendoza, Rev. Felix Ruh,
Rev. Efrain Alvarado, Sr. Miguel Calvetti, women elder, Rev.
C.A. Phillips; Front row: Rev. Antonio Piccardo, Rev.B.B.Shiflett,
Sr. Manuel Key. (John H. Sinclair took the photo).

VENEZUELAN PROVERBS

"Camaron que se duerme, se le lleva la corriente"

  The shrimp that goes to sleep is swept away by the stream:

"El que trabaja, no come paja"

  He who works does not eat straw.

"Gallo que no canta, algo tiene en la garganta"

  The rooster who doesn't crow has something in its throat.

"En casa de carpintero tiene cama hecha de cuero"

  In the carpenter's home, the bed is made of leather.

"La cruz en el pecho y el Diablo en el hecho"

  The cross is on the breast, but the Devil is in the deed.

"Quién no oye consejos, no llega a viejo"

  The one who does not accept advice, never will get old.

"Bueno es cilantro, pero no tanto"

  The corlander is good, but not too much of it.

"Quién mantiene el pico, ya se hace rico"

  The one who keeps his mouth shut, already has become rich.

SUPERSTITIONES AND FOLKLORE

"Tiene un sambenito" is to place the blame or to be a 'con' man.

"Tiene cara de Pascua"' is to put on a show of generosity

Santa Tecla (tecla refers to the musical key) is to tell it like it is or "hit the nail on the head".

"Las de San Quintín" is to cause a *"lío"* or a mess. San Quintín is the saint who messes things up!

DEFINITION OF ISOLATION

The reference is to "Paracotos", a very remote village in the State of Miranda. *"Ni se oye en Paracotos" o Se arruninó Paracotos, pero salvó el pais"* (Cf. Salas, p. 17)

PRAYERS TO THE SAINTS.

When confronted by an angry dog: "San Marcos de León, calm my heart".

If confronted by a snake: "San Marcos Bendito, save me from that poisonous one"

If afraid of "the evil eye" (mal de ojo) " En el nombre de San Luis Beltran, save me from the curse of the evil eye"

If the weather is threatening "Santa Clara, que se aclare"

DEFINITIONS of a bar or a saloon

" La taberna" es for the aristocrats; "La cantina" is for the public; "El café" - is the restaurant; "la bodega" is the store; "la pulperia" es the "roadside snack bar".

A FOUR WEEK BOOK STUDY PLAN

First Week -   Part One

The differences and similarities in the histories of North America and Latin America and the Caribbean.

Scripture readings: Psalm 67, Isaiah 2: 1-4; Matthew 28:16-20
Acts of the Apostles 1: 1-8
What is unique about the history of Venezuela in comparison with other countries in Latin America and the Caribbean?
What changes have come in Venezuela in the past two decades?

Second Week – Parts Two and Three

How are the stories of Ramón and Maria and Antonio and Mary similar?
How are these stories different?
Which one of the neighbors would you like to know better? Why?
How is your own faith journey like one of these characters?
Scripture readings: Psalm 72; Isaiah 42: 1-12; Matthew 9:35 – 10:23;
      Acts 10.

Third week - Parts Four and Five

What did you learn from the outreach of the Santa Barbara congregation? How is it relevant to your local congregation?

Scripture readings: Isaiah 60: John 4: 1-20; Acts 10: 6-40

Fourth week   Parts Six and Seven

Scripture readings: John 17: Ephesians 3: Jonah 3-4; Isaiah 49: 1-13

A general question for each session

Think about the persons for whom you are thankful and the reasons for your gratitude. The early church seemed to include in their letters references to special people who meant a great deal to their spiritual development..

MORE DISCUSSION QUESTIONS

1. John Sinclair's ambition in writing RAMON, MARY AND THEIR NEIGHBORS was "to tell an old-fashioned, truth-telling story" What essential human truths does it convey?

2. What do these stories reveal about the emotional lives of missionaries? Are they changed by the work they do?

3. What do these stories tell the reader about the roles of compassion, faith and hope in the work of the missionary?

4. How does the author use the details of the political unrest in Venezuela to create tension and surprise?

5. How does Ramón ("Suro") develop as a church leader during his life?

6. Is there any real connection between "spiritual renewal" and "authentic democracy" in the development of political change?

7. What new understanding of mission did you learn from reading this book?

THE PHOTOGRAPHS AND THE PHOTOGRAPHER

I am indebted to Richard L. Turner, Jr. for most of the excellent photos which provide the reader with visual images of the people and their life in rural Venezuela in the 1950s.

"Rich" Turner was a close friend since 1944 when he was a student at the Drexel Institute of Technology in Philadelphia and I was studying at Princeton Theological Seminary. My wife and I were recently married and were"adopted" by the Turner family as "their Eastern children" during those years.

In the school year, 1953-54, he served as a volunteer missionary teacher in the Bello Monte High School in Caracas, Venezuela. This is a ediucational institution of the Presbyterian Church. During that year, he traveled with the author to remote rural areas and captured with his camera the memorable and poignant photographs which illuminate the text. Before his death in September, 2011 he gave permission to use his photographs to illustrate the stories in FAITH AND FREEDOM.

Richard Turner studied electrical engineering, and earned a Ph.D. in that field from the University of Washington in 1963. He served in the E.E. department of Seattle University from 1963 – 1993. At the time of his retirement he was awarded the title of "professor emeritus".

Together with his wife, Sonia, they reared their two children, Kristen and Allyn. They were active in the Presbyterian churches in the Seattle area for many years. Richard was ordained a ruling elder in 1961. Dr. Turner was an exemplary Christian layman, a devoted husband and father and an outstanding professional educator.

Three additional photographs were taken by Leon V. Kofod, a professional photographer who was employed by the former Board of Foreign Missions of the Presbyterian Church, USA, to document Presbyterian mission work in Latin America in the early 1950s. Other photographs were taken by the author during the years of his service in Venezuela, 1949 – 1956.

FE DE ERRATA

Iii "...new ideas as threatning..."
p. 3 "Venezuela suffered initially..."
p. 5 "...and pay the annual quiota..."
p. 58 "...did not need formal pedagodical..."
p. 66 spelling of 'Babel"
p. 72 "...in an official national census..."
p. 100 "...joined Josefina de Rivero and..."
p. 155 "THE TIME OF OUR LIVES"
p. 169 "An educational institution of..."
p. 157 "Rev. Alvin and Mrs.(Pauline) Schutmaat